SpringerBriefs in Computer Science

Series Editors

Stan Zdonik, Brown University
Providence, RI, USA

Shashi Shekhar, University of Minnesota
Minneapolis, MN, USA

Xindong Wu, University of Vermont
Burlington, VT, USA

Lakhmi C. Jain, University of South Australia
Adelaide, SA, Australia

David Padua, University of Illinois Urbana-Champaign
Urbana, IL, USA

Xuemin Sherman Shen, University of Waterloo
Waterloo, ON, Canada

Borko Furht, Florida Atlantic University
Boca Raton, FL, USA

V. S. Subrahmanian, University of Maryland
College Park, MD, USA

Martial Hebert, Carnegie Mellon University
Pittsburgh, PA, USA

Katsushi Ikeuchi, University of Tokyo
Tokyo, Japan

Bruno Siciliano, Università di Napoli Federico II
Napoli, Italy

Sushil Jajodia, George Mason University
Fairfax, VA, USA

Newton Lee, Institute for Education, Research and Scholarships
Los Angeles, CA, USA

SpringerBriefs present concise summaries of cutting-edge research and practical applications across a wide spectrum of fields. Featuring compact volumes of 50 to 125 pages, the series covers a range of content from professional to academic.

Typical topics might include:

- A timely report of state-of-the art analytical techniques
- A bridge between new research results, as published in journal articles, and a contextual literature review
- A snapshot of a hot or emerging topic
- An in-depth case study or clinical example
- A presentation of core concepts that students must understand in order to make independent contributions

Briefs allow authors to present their ideas and readers to absorb them with minimal time investment. Briefs will be published as part of Springer's eBook collection, with millions of users worldwide. In addition, Briefs will be available for individual print and electronic purchase. Briefs are characterized by fast, global electronic dissemination, standard publishing contracts, easy-to-use manuscript preparation and formatting guidelines, and expedited production schedules. We aim for publication 8–12 weeks after acceptance. Both solicited and unsolicited manuscripts are considered for publication in this series.

**Indexing: This series is indexed in Scopus, Ei-Compendex, and zbMATH **

More information about this series at https://link.springer.com/bookseries/10028

Hermann Kopetz

Data, Information, and Time

The DIT Model

 Springer

Hermann Kopetz (iD)
Institute of Computer Engineering
(emeritus), Vienna University of Technology
Vienna, Austria

ISSN 2191-5768   ISSN 2191-5776   (electronic)
SpringerBriefs in Computer Science
ISBN 978-3-030-96328-6   ISBN 978-3-030-96329-3   (eBook)
https://doi.org/10.1007/978-3-030-96329-3

This Springer imprint is published by the registered company Springer Nature Switzerland AG
The registered company address is: Gewerbestrasse 11, 6330 Cham, Switzerland

Foreword

In this interesting and challenging work, Herman Kopetz introduces his Data-Information-and-Time (DIT) model, which is a comprehensive and intriguingly elegant model of truth, communication, and meaning, parameterized by time instants of an absolute and ubiquitous real time. The author, Hermann Kopetz, is somebody who definitely knows his topic as an internationally highly respected top Computer Scientist and expert on real-time systems and as the main founder of TTTech, a world-leading provider of real-time solutions to the automotive and aviation industries.

The DIT model explains the difference between data and information according to the *signifier-signified* paradigm of Semiotics and gives a modern explication and formalization of the notion of the "signified" through the introduction of the notion of *information item*, abbreviated by *itom*. An itom is essentially a simple phrase with a clear meaning at any given point in time. The meaning of an itom is determined by its inner context, roughly, the activated brain patterns and its outer context, which are, roughly, the external circumstances, laws, social norms, and states of affair. The DIT model is put in relation with theories of brain science and with important fields of Computer Science, such as the Semantic Web and Real-Time Systems. The work is clear cut and illuminating. It will serve as a reference to many authors investigating related topics.

University of Oxford   Georg Gottlob
Oxford, UK

Preface

The idea of gaining an understanding of the relationships between the fundamental terms *data and information* to *time* has been part of my thinking for many years. In 1979 I attended the *Newcastle Seminar on Teaching of Computer Science* [1], organized by *Brian Randell*, and listened to an inspiring lecture by *William Kent* on the *Future Requirements of Data Modelling*. This excellent lecture, and the subsequent study of Kent's interesting book on *Data and Reality* [2], raised more questions than answers about the *meaning of a data item* and the *sense*, i.e., *the idea* that is communicated by a natural language sentence or by the result of a database query.

In most of my career I worked with *real-time computer systems*. In a real-time control system an observation of the physical environment can only be used for the control of a real-world physical process within a limited interval of physical time. There is thus the need for a model that explains the relationships among data, information, and the flow of physical time. I soon realized that the conception of such a model requires a much wider view than that provided within the silo of computer science. Only after I have moved to the state of an emeritus I found the time to pore over the domains of linguistics, cognition, philosophy, and the biological structure of our brain that are important if one wants to understand the relations among data, information, and time in depth.

This work aims to present a model—I call it the *data-information-and-time (DIT) model*—that clarifies the semantics behind the terms *data, information,* and their relations to the *passage of real time*. According to the DIT model *a data item* is a symbol the signifier of which appears as a *pattern* (e.g., visual, sound, gesture, or any bit pattern) in physical space. The *signifier* of the symbol is generated by a human or a machine in the *current contextual situation* and is linked to a concept in the human mind or a set of operations of a machine as its *signified. An information item* delivers the *sense* or the *idea* that a human mind extracts out of a given natural language proposition that is composed of meaningful *data items*. Since the given tangible, intangible, and temporal context are part of the *explanation* of a data item, a change of context can have an effect on the meaning of data and the sense of a proposition. The DIT model provides a framework to show how the *flow of time* can change the truth-value of a proposition. I compare the notions of *data, information,* and *time* in differing contexts: in human communication, in the operation of a computer system, and in a biological system. In the final Section I present a few simple examples to demonstrate how the lessons learned from the DIT model can help to improve the design of a computer system.

Many discussions within the IFIP WG 10.4, in particular with John Rushby and Brian Randell, have created an important impetus to go ahead with this work. Special thanks go to Thomas Eiter, Frank Furrer, Georg Gottlob, Radu Grosu, Wilfried Steiner, and Neeraj Suri, who have provided very helpful comments to an earlier version of this work. My special thanks go to Paul Drougas, Senior Editor of Springer Nature, who supported this project in a most constructive way.

Vienna, Austria   Hermann Kopetz
January 2022

Contents

Chapter 1
Introduction

The terms *data and information* refer to core concepts in the domain of information technology. They are central and widely used terms in any conversation about the evolving information society. Colloquially, these words are used in a variety of different situations without much concern for the precise meaning that is communicated by these terms. Some uses of these terms assume that they are *synonyms*, while other uses consider that these two terms have *different* meanings, but fail to identify the key differences between them. Even in the scientific community, the precise *semantics* that is carried by these terms is not agreed upon [3].

Since ambiguous terminology threatens to cloud the understanding and, in consequence, the progress of a scientific field, the meaning of these core terms is widely discussed in the technical, scientific, and philosophical literature. Capurro [4, pp. 195–268] provides a good overview of the etymology of the term *information* and points out that the term *information* has very different meanings in different communities. Dretske [5] and Bates [6] present new theories of information, but do not consider that a data item can change its meaning as time progresses. The most cited theory of information, *Claude Shannon's mathematical theory of information* [7, 8], studies the fundamental limits of signal transmission and data compression across a transmission line. Colin Cherry, in his book on *Human Communication*, remarks [9, p. 9]: "*As a theory it* (Shannon's mathematical theory of information) *lies at the syntactic level of sign theory and is abstracted from the semantic and pragmatic level.*" Shannon once remarked that "*it is hardly to be expected that a single concept of information would satisfactorily account for the numerous possible applications of this general field*" [10, p. 180].

It is the objective of this work to present a model—we call it the *DIT model*—that clarifies the semantics behind the terms *information* and *data* and their relations to the passage of *time*. It provides a framework to show how the *flow of time* affects the meaning of *stored data* and can change the truth-value of a proposition. According to the DIT model a *data item* is a *symbol* that consists of a *signifier* and a *signified*. The signifier of *a data item* is a pattern (e.g., visual, sound, gesture, word, or any bit

H. Kopetz, *Data, Information, and Time*, SpringerBriefs in Computer Science,
https://doi.org/10.1007/978-3-030-96329-3_1

1

pattern) in physical space that is generated by a human or a machine in the current contextual situation. The *signified* of a meaningful *data item* is a concept in the mind of a human. An *information item,* an *Itom,* provides the *sense—the idea—*that a human mind extracts out of a given proposition consisting of a sequence of meaningful data items. Since the given tangible, intangible, and temporal contexts are part of the *explanation* of a data item, a change of context can have an effect on the *meaning* of data and the *sense* of a proposition.

The views on the concepts *information, data,* and *time* that are the basis for this work have been influenced by the insights gained from the works of Bar-Hillel and Carnap [11], Floridi [12], Frege [13], Kent [2], Lyon [14], Mealy [15], and Wittgenstein [16] on *semantic information,* by Popper's paper on *Three Worlds* [17], by the work of Edelman and Tononi [18], Koch and Crick [19], and Rushby [20] on *consciousness*, and by the publications of Johnson [21] and Lakoff [22] on *embodied cognition.*

This work is structured as follows: In Chap. 2, we provide a short overview of the key ideas of the DIT model. Chapter 3 explains the fundamental terms used in this work and presents our view of the world that is based on *scientific realism.* The work adopts the Newtonian time model that posits an absolute timeline that extends from the past to the future. The notions of an *entity*, a *category*, a *symbol*, and a *model* are discussed in detail. Chapter 4 is devoted to the important role that the *context* plays in the generation and explanation of data. It distinguishes between the *outer context* of a conversation that is part of the social and cultural environment and the *inner context* in the minds of a speaker and listener of an utterance. Chapter 5 elaborates on the *meaning of words* and the structure of natural language. It distinguishes between the *semantic meaning* and the *denotational meaning* of a proposition and introduces the concept of an *information item*, abbreviated by *Itom*, that captures the *sense* of a proposition. Chapter 6 presents the details of the DIT model in oral and written communication among humans. It elaborates the notion of *stigmergic communication* and discusses the meaning of data in cyberspace. Chapter 7 focusses on archival computer systems. It first explains the central role of the *schema* of a data structure for the explanation of the meaning of a data item. It then introduces DIT knowledge graphs as means to visualize the dependence relations and the timing among entities. The final part of Chap. 7 contains a short discussion about the Semantic Net and big data analytics. Chapter 8 is devoted to the role of Itoms in real-time control systems. At first it clarifies some control system terminology on four short examples of real-time control systems. It then elaborates on the conflict between timeliness and precision of real-time data and introduces the notion of an anytime algorithm to solve this conflict. The final part of Chap. 8 describes the fundamental differences between a semiautonomous and a fully autonomous safety-critical real-time control system. Chapter 9 deals with data in biological systems. It considers the genome as a *control database* for the growth of an organism and compares the use of the term *data item* in computer systems, the growth of a plant, and in human communication. Chapter 10 focusses on the *generation* and *explanation* of data and explains how the progression of time between the instants of *data generation* and *data retrieval* can change the meaning of a data item and the truth-value of a proposition. In Chap. 11 we present a few simple examples to demonstrate how the insights gained from the DIT model can help to improve the design of a computer system. The work closes with a conclusion in Chap. 12. The glossary in the appendix provides explications of some of the technical terms used in this book.

Chapter 2
Overview of the DIT Model

The Data, Information and Time (DIT) Model provides a clarification of the differences in the meaning of the terms *data* and *information* and explains the communication among humans through the use of natural language propositions. It examines how a proposition can change its *sense* as time progresses.

The DIT model is based on the position of sc*ientific realism*, a position that posits that *reality* exists independently of an observer [23]. A human starts to learn about reality by the inputs from the human senses and the observations of the effects of her/his motor actions. She/he acquires language by communicating with other humans, in the beginning nonverbally and later verbally in a given cultural context. Using the direct inputs from the human senses and explanations from other humans formulated in natural language, she/he builds internal subjective *mental models* of the world in her/his mind and acquires the meaning of new natural language words.

A *mental model* consists of *concepts* and *relations among concepts*. A concept is a *unit of thought* [24] that can refer to a specific *thing* (e.g., *a person*), a *construct*, or a *relation*. Every concept is related to a plethora of other concepts. The totality of all concepts, relations among the concepts, and mental models forms the *conceptual landscape* in the mind of a human that is built up during the lifetime of an individual, partly by *human nature* and partly by *nurture,* i.e., the lived and remembered personal experiences. Each fully developed concept has a rich set of *conscious* and *unconscious (tacit)* relations to other concepts in the conceptual landscape. Boulding [25] calls the conceptual landscape the *Image*.

Communication among humans and of a human with a machine is primarily realized by the use of *natural language*. A sentence in a natural language consists of a structured sequence of words or phrases. Every word or word phrase is embodied in reality as a sound stream or as written text of language symbols in the given cultural context. In the DIT model a *data item* is a symbol. In human communication the signifier of the symbol is the physical embodiment of a word. The *signified* of the symbol—the meaning of the word—is a concept in the mind of the human. The meaning of a word is on one side determined by the *outer context*, i.e., the common

H. Kopetz, *Data, Information, and Time*, SpringerBriefs in Computer Science,
https://doi.org/10.1007/978-3-030-96329-3_2

use of the word in the language community (the *denotation* of the word) and on the other side by the *inner context*, i.e., the subjective associations of the word in the conceptual landscape (the mind) of a human sender or receiver (we call these subjective associations that go beyond the *denotation of a word* the *connotations of a word*).

In the DIT model we call a basic natural language sentence that consists of three-word phrases, a *subject phrase*, a *predicate phrase* and an *object phrase,* a *proposition*. Given that the words used in the proposition have an established meaning in the mind of the listener, the *predicate* of the proposition establishes a link between the concept denoted by the *subject* and the concept denoted by the *object*. In the DIT model we call the *sense* of a natural language proposition an *information item (Itom)*. *Words* have an (isolated) meaning, but the compound of a natural language sentence communicates an *idea*—the *sense* of the sentence.

In natural language, the predicate of a proposition discloses temporal information by the use of a tense. There are 12 tenses in English [26] that are related to the placement of the proposition on the timeline and express temporal relations. In the DIT model we do not use the tense system to express temporal relations, but assign temporal parameters to the predicate of a proposition to inform the listener during what times the proposition is assumed to hold.

In a computer program the signifier of a *data item* is a *token name* (e.g., the name of a *variable* in a program) or a *literal*. The *signified* of a token name is a *token*, i.e., a *meaningless placeholder* from the world of *constructs* that can hold a value and can take part in a set of computations. At the human/computer interface the tokens must be grounded by the replacement of the token names by natural language words that are meaningful to the prospective user.

Chapter 3
Fundamental Terms

In this chapter we outline our world model and describe the meaning of important terms that are used throughout this work. The glossary at the end of this book summarizes the explanations of important terms that are used throughout this work.

3.1 Time and Space

The DIT model is based on the *Newtonian model of time* and maps the progression of time to an *absolute timeline* that extends from the past to the future. When we talk of a *timeline* we are making use of the *space-time analogy* [27]. We call a cut of the timeline an *instant* and a section of the timeline a *duration*. The instant *now,* the *present,* partitions the timeline into two unbounded segments, the *past* and the *future*.

A *digital clock* is a device that periodically produces instants, called the *ticks of the clock* that print a regular pattern on the timeline from the past up to the instant *now*. The section between two consecutive ticks of a digital clock is called the *granularity* of the clock. We assume that the ticks of the clock are *numbered* and *synchronized* with an external time standard, such as UTC (Universal Time Coordinated) that is distributed by the GPS (Global Positioning System). GPS provides a standardized worldwide distribution system for the numbering of the ticks of a UTC clock. The finest granularity that is supported by GPS is better than 100 ns.

The granularity of a digital clock entails an unavoidable *accuracy error* in time measurement that is extensively discussed in [28, pp. 51–77]. When we build a model of the behavior of a system, we have to choose a clock with a granularity that agrees with the dynamics of the system that is modeled, such that *accuracy errors* can be regarded as second-order quantities that can be neglected. For example, in some technical systems a *millisecond* may be an appropriate granularity, while in an archeological system the appropriate granularity can be a *year*.

H. Kopetz, *Data, Information, and Time*, SpringerBriefs in Computer Science,
https://doi.org/10.1007/978-3-030-96329-3_3

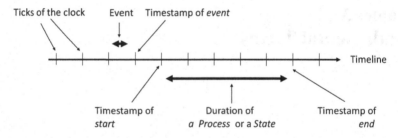

Fig. 3.1 Timestamps of events, processes, and states

A process is an activity that starts at the instant *start_of_process* and terminates at the instant *end_of_process* (Fig. 3.1). If the duration between *start_of_process* and *end_of_process* is smaller than the chosen granularity of the clock, we call the activity an *event*. The time value—we call it the *timestamp*—that is assigned to an event is the *tick number* that immediately follows the *end_of_process* (Fig. 3.1). (Note that the temporal order of a set of events can only be established on the basis of their timestamps if this set is *sparse*—see ref. [29]). If a process lasts longer than a granule of the chosen clock, then we introduce the concept of an *interval* that is placed on the timeline and delimited by two *events*, i.e., two different timestamps.

If the properties of a phenomenon that is of relevance in our investigations have constant values (i.e., do not change) during an interval, then we say that the phenomenon is in the *state* defined by these properties during this interval. A state is thus delimited by two events, the *start of state* and the *end of state*.

In the DIT model we assume the availability of a function *GPST(now)* that provides the UTC value of the *timestamp* of the event *now* at the instant of executing the function.

In this work we use the following *decimal notation* to define the syntax for a full timestamp with a resolution of a microsecond, referring to UTC time:

$$\langle\text{year}\rangle\langle\text{month}\rangle\langle\text{day}\rangle\langle\text{hour}\rangle\langle\text{minute}\rangle\langle\text{second}\rangle\langle\text{millisecond}\rangle\langle\text{microsecond}\rangle$$

An example of such a *full timestamp* is:

$$2021\ 08\ 03\ 12\ 54\ 36\ 233\ 788$$

If a *prefix* of a full timestamp is obvious from the context and a *postfix* of a full timestamp is smaller than the chosen granularity, then this *prefix* and *postfix* can be omitted to arrive at an *ordinary timestamp*, or *timestamp* for short.

For example, if the year is *obvious* and the *chosen granularity is 1 h,* the above *full timestamp* would be reduced to

2021 **08 03 12** 54 36 233 788

Such a *timestamp* denotes unambiguously the time on the standardized UTC timeline. This can be the point of occurrence of an event or the *starting point* or *the termination point* of an interval.

In the DIT model we use the term *happening* as an umbrella term that includes an *event*, a *state*, or a *process*. If a happening denotes an *event*, then a single time-stamp is sufficient to characterize the temporal aspect. If the happening denotes a *state* or a *process*, then two timestamps are required.

3.2   Entities, Properties, and Categories

In this section we clarify some terms that are frequently used in the rest of this work.

Entity   In the DIT model a *unit of consideration* is called an *entity*. An entity can be *an animate or inanimate thing* that exists in reality or a *construct*, an intangible product of the human mind [17].

Considered Space-Time Domain   In order to restrict the number of entities that must be considered in a deliberation, the notion of a *considered space-time domain (CSTD)* is introduced in the DIT model. The CSTD constrains an external physical environment to a subspace of the four-dimensional space-time domain delimited by the *Universe of Discourse (UoD)* and the *Interval of Discourse (IoD)*. The *Universe of Discourse* comprises the *set of entities* and the relations among the entities in the considered environment. The *Interval of Discourse (IoD)* restricts the considered interval on the timeline.

Property   An entity has a large number of *properties*, i.e., characteristic features. Take the example of a simple thing, such as a *stone*. A stone can be characterized by the properties of weight, form, hardness, color, composition, temperature, and many more. We distinguish between *static* properties and dynamic properties of an entity in the given IoD. *Static properties* are constant in the IoD, while *dynamic properties* can change during the IoD. For example, the weight of a stone is normally a *static property*, while the *temperature* of a stone is a *dynamic property*.

Value   In the DIT model we call the further characterization of a *property* of a thing a *value*. For example, the temperature of a stone can be characterized at a chosen instant in time by a *numerical value* of *measurement units*, such as degrees Celsius. A value of a dynamic property requires the recording of the instant in time, when the value has been observed (since the value can change with the progression of time in the IoD). A value can be a numeric value or an alphanumeric value (e.g., the name of a color). A *sole value* without an explanation, i.e., without an indication of the meaning of the value and the measurements units that are used to record a numerical value, is most often of no use.

Category A *category* is a *set of entities* that share a number of chosen *static properties* and carries a *name*. (In data modeling, a *category* is often called a *class*.) It is a *construct* that encompasses cognate entities or lower-level categories that are characterized by common properties. Each category is formed for a given purpose in order to *simplify thinking and communication*. The purpose of a category determines the properties that are characteristic of the entities in the chosen category. For example, an entity that is used by a sculptor for the purpose of making a sculpture and is composed of *metamorphosed lime* is called a *marble stone*. *Marble stone* is thus a *subset* of the category *stone* or the category *stone* is a *superset* of the category *marble stone*. A category can be specified by naming necessary properties that a member of a category must possess or by naming a prototype of a characteristic exemplar of the category. In some cases, membership to a category is *fuzzy*, if the entity of the category is at a wide distance from the identifying characteristic prototype. A fuzzy member of a category can give rise to misunderstandings in communication.

System The term *system* is used at many places in this book. We work with the following definition of the term *system* [30, p. 129]:

A system is a collection of related entities that forms a whole.

The *wholeness* is a defining characteristic of a system. In many cases, a system is enclosed by a type of a *skin* that separates the system from its environment. Identifiable entities inside a system are often called *subsystems*, *parts*, or *components* of the system. The static relationship among the parts inside the system is called the *structure of the system*. The entities in the CSTD that are not part of the system but have the capability to interact with the system during the IoD are called the *environment of a system*. A system and its environment interact by *interfaces* that are located in the *skin* of the system. The skin with its interfaces thus forms a *boundary* between the system and its environment. An external entity in the CSTD can only interact with a system, if *some property of the external entity* can be *observed* by a sensor or *influenced* by an actuator of the system. The environment that is noticed by a system thus depends on the sensing and actuating capability of the system. A system may be *sensitive to the progression of time,* implying that the system may react differently at different points in time. Take as an example a heating system in a home that maintains a different temperature during the day from the temperature during the night.

3.3   Symbols

The notion of a *symbol* takes a central position in human thinking and the construction of a model. A symbol consists of two parts

- A *signifier,* i.e., a *physical pattern* that represents the symbol in the physical world and.
- The *signified* that is *the something* the signifier stands for.

The *signifier of a symbol* can be a picture, a sound, a gesture, a letter, a digit, a word, or any kind of *physical pattern* that stands for *something*. The *signifier of a symbol* is also called the *name of the symbol* that identifies the *something*. According to Wikipedia, "*A name is a term used for identification. A name can identify a class or category of entities, or a single entity, either uniquely, or within a given context.*"

Depending on what a signifier stands for, in human communication we distinguish between four types of signifiers in the DIT model:

1. a proper name,
2. a token name,
3. a literal,
4. a word of a natural language.

A *proper name* is a signifier that has a *unique entity* as its signified, e.g., a specific person or a unique entity in the world of the given CSTD. This unique entity is sometimes called a *referent*. We thus say that a *proper name* is *grounded* in reality.

A *token name* denotes a *token*, i.e., a *meaningless placeho*lder in the world of *constructs* that can hold a value and can take part in a set of relations. A set of tokens and their specified relations form a *token system*. The tokens of a token system are related to each other, i.e., each meaningless placeholder is related to other meaningless placeholders, but not to entities in the real world. The problem of how to assign meaning to the tokens of a token system, i.e., assign meaningful natural language words to the placeholders, is called the *Symbol Grounding Problem* [31].

The term *grounding* denotes the assignment of meaningful words to meaningless tokens.

A signifier is a *literal*, if the *gestalt* of the signifier indicates unambiguously the signified in the given cultural environment. A good example for a literal is a string of digits (the *signifier*) that denotes a *numerical value* (the *signified*) in a numeral system. The decimal numeral system introduces ten different *gestalts* (the digits from 0 to 9) to denote the numerical values of the first ten *numbers*. Arbitrarily large *numerical values* can be represented by a string of decimal digits. The *something* of such a string of digits is the designated *numerical value*.

A *word* of a given natural language denotes a *formed concept* in the mind of a human that is part of the language community. We discuss the difficult problem of how to ground the meaning of a word in a given natural language in the Section on *language and information*.

3.4   Models

A *model* of a real-world phenomenon provides an *abstraction* of reality. An abstraction is a *simplification* that leaves out the many details of a scenario that are not considered relevant for the given purpose of the model [30]. The given purpose provides the point of view that determines which properties of the scenario must be part of the model. A crystal clear description of the purpose of a model is therefore the starting point for model building.

A *mental model* of an observed phenomenon often provides an *explanation* for the recognized phenomenon [32, p. 419]. Kenneth Craik outlines the three basic steps that are required to build a mental model [33, p. 50] of an *external process:* " ' *(i) Translation' of the external process into words, numbers and other symbols. (ii) Arrival at other symbols by a process of 'reasoning', deduction, inference etc., and (iii) 'Retranslation' of these symbols into external processes.*" The execution of the mental model provides mental *simulation results* that are compared with the *physical results* of the modeled external process. If these results are *compatible*, a faithful mental model has been reached that provides an *explanation* for the behavior of the external process.

A *model* can be used for explanation, understanding, or prediction of the behavior of a real-world phenomenon. *Explanation* and *understanding* are closely related. If we can *explain* a phenomenon, we *understand* the phenomenon and if we *understand* a phenomenon, we can *explain* it. There are different levels of understanding and explanation, depending on the subjective knowledge base (i.e., the conceptual landscape) that is available in the mind of a human. An expert in a field, who has developed a set of refined concepts in the area of her/his expertise can provide a much more detailed and scientifically sound explanation than a layman [34, p. 14].

A model that can provide a *prediction* of the behavior of a phenomenon does not necessarily provide an *explanation* of the phenomenon. Take the example of an opaque model that consists of a multi-level deep neural network consisting of thousands of artificial neurons. The many parameters of the neural network are set during an extensive training phase. The logical coherence of the model, which is a prerequisite for understanding the model, cannot be established by examining the thousands of parameters that have been set in the training phase.

Chapter 4
Context

In human communication the *meaning* of a natural language word depends on the *context* and the time *of the conversation*. The Collins Dictionary defines *context* as follows: *"The context of an idea or event is the general situation that relates to it, and which helps it to be understood."* The *context* consists not only of the spatial and temporal environment of the utterance per se but also of the preceding discourse that can have an effect on the precise meanings of the employed words.

In the following sections we distinguish between the *inner context* in the mind of the human speaker or listener and the *outer context* of the representation of the *word* in the physical world.

4.1 Inner Context

The *inner context* of the meaning of a word in the mind of a conscious human consists of

- those parts of the conceptual landscape in the human brain that are related to the meaning of the word and,
- the current perceptions of relevant events in the physical environment, i.e., the outer context, that are delivered to the conceptual landscape by the human senses.

The following analysis of the *inner context* of an Itom is based on the *Theory of Neuronal Group Selection*, called the TNGS theory of human consciousness, developed by Edelman and Tononi [18]. Although this TNGS theory of human consciousness is still widely debated in the research community, it provides a reasonable framework for the explanation of consciousness as an *emergent property* as a consequence of the intense interactions among a very large number of neurons in the human brain.

© The Author(s), under exclusive license to Springer Nature Switzerland AG 2022
H. Kopetz, *Data, Information, and Time*, SpringerBriefs in Computer Science,
https://doi.org/10.1007/978-3-030-96329-3_4

Central to the TNGS theory is the *dynamic core hypothesis* that posits that at any instant *consciousness* is embodied by an integrated cluster of neurons, called the *dynamic core*, composed of millions of highly interactive neurons in a special area (the thalamocortical system) of the human brain. The composition of this dynamic core can change rapidly as the *human attention* shifts from one topic to another topic and requires access to a different part of the conceptual landscape. The *attention shift time* is in the order of *hundreds of milliseconds*. The dynamic core has access to episodic and linguistic memory and can support rational thoughts about the past, the present, and the future.

The dynamic core, which is the *neural correlate of consciousness*, carries out a single sequential conscious neural process at any one time. It interacts with the other areas of the brain, where a plethora of powerful concurrent autonomous neural processes are active, by *input ports* and *output ports*.

The current perceptions of the physical environment are preprocessed and categorized by sophisticated autonomous neural processes before they are delivered in the form of a *high-level concept* to an input port of the dynamic core. For example, the inputs to human vision that are provided by the different types of photoreceptive cells of the two eyes are fused and categorized by powerful autonomous neural processes in the vision subsystem before the high-level result, let us say a *car on a road*, is given to the dynamic core. We must already know what a *car on a road* could look like before we can recognize a *car on a road*. The same applies to the output port, where a high-level command, such as a command for the generation of speech, is handed over to autonomous neural circuits that control the detailed motor outputs to the muscles of the larynx in order to realize the intended sound pattern in the physical environment.

According to the TNGS theory *consciousness* is an *emergent phenomenon* that arises when the neurons of the dynamic core interact intensely. Consciousness is a first-person subjective experience [35, p. 20] that supervenes on the biological activities of the neurons in the dynamic core.

In another work [36], Edelman has considered the available evidence about the evolution of the brain in the animal kingdom over the past hundreds of millions of years, building on Darwin's theory of *The Origin of Species* [37]. In this work Edelman found out that the dynamic core that enables the development of language and conscious thinking about past and future events by using symbols is a recent addition in the history of the evolution of the brain. Most of the essential brain functions that support the sustenance of life are carried out by autonomous processes of the human brain and only those parameters of the human body that can have an effect on the willed human behavior are made available to the dynamic core. For example, the dynamic core is aware of the feeling of pain, but not of high blood pressure. When we fall asleep, the dynamic core becomes kind of inactive, while other autonomous processes continue to function and control the vital parameters of life.

The border line between the conscious processes in the dynamic core and the autonomous processes in the rest of the brain is modified by learning, practice, and experience. For example, when learning a new sport or a new musical instrument, in the starting phase detailed motor commands are generated by a conscious process in the dynamic core. After some practice, a more abstract command by the dynamic core suffices to start a sequence of autonomous neural processes that produce a succession of detailed motor commands.

The same growth process of autonomous neural subsystems takes place at the input side of the dynamic core. An expert that looks regularly at a phenomenon will immediately realize a deviation from the normal state without having to go through a sequence of rational analysis steps.

Frequent use of a set of neurons changes the association patterns among the neurons and stimulates the growth of new neurons, such that a new autonomous subsystem of neurons for the execution of a learned task emerges. *Neurons that are frequently fired together will eventually be wired together.*

Over time, the physical structure of the human brain is modified by its usage.

The *inner context* of a word is thus determined by the dynamic core that is associated with this word at a given instant and by the rational and tacit links of the neurons in this dynamic core to a plethora of neurons of associated autonomous neural processes. Since the dynamic core includes access to linguistic memory, the translation of an idea to a verbal formulation in the form of a proposition, i.e., the selection of words (the signifiers) that represent the *sense of the proposition,* the *Itom,* in the chosen language, is performed in the linguistic memory and the dynamic core with no or little mental effort.

4.2   Outer Context

The *outer context* of a *word* or an *action* is the objective reality in the current situation. It is determined by the prevailing physical, cultural, and social environment.

We call the totality of static values of the properties of entities in *the considered space-time domain* (CSTD) *context data* (*c-data*) of the *outer context*, while the values of the dynamic properties of entities that are of relevance in a given communication act are called *essential data (e-data)*. What is of relevance is determined by the *intentions* of the speaker. If the *inner contexts* of all interacting humans were perfectly aligned with the *outer context* of the CSTD, then there would be no need to communicate c-data in a conversation, because all involved humans have a properly aligned inner context. However, a perfect alignment of the inner and outer context at the start of a conversation is highly unlikely, since a partner might not know which entities and which properties of the entities in the CSTD are of interest to the other partner. Therefore, the partners must first agree on the set of entities and properties that are of relevance to satisfy their intentions. Such an inner context alignment of the partners requires the exchange of *c-data.*

Look at the following example: In ancient times the Itom *"an enemy is approaching"* was transmitted by the incineration of a fire on a selected hill, thus encoding the vital single bit—the *e-data*—in the appearance of a pre-arranged fire in the physical environment. The associated c-data, i.e., the context for the interpretation of the appearance of fire on the selected hill has been arranged by a social agreement ahead of time and does not change in the *outer context* of the *e-data* during the CSTD.

The cultural environment of the outer context of an Itom is determined by the social behavior, the use of language, the laws, the accepted social norms, and the customs and manners of the *clientele of an Itom*. The knowledge and the capabilities of the *clientele of an Itom* provide the background for the explanation of the meaning of words that are used to represent the Itom. At the moment, when the representation of an Itom—the words—for the given outer world is chosen by the dynamic core of the sender, the *inner context* of the sender and the shared *outer context* should be well aligned. The same holds for the other side, the receiver of the Itom, who must interpret the signifiers—the words—of the Itom.

The human senses provide the means to align the *inner context* with a changing *outer context*.

Normally the meaning of a word remains static in the CSTD, although the denotation of a word in a language community can change slowly over history. The physical and the cultural environments are normally changing in the CSTD, effecting a modification of the outer context and—if the considered IoD is many years—even a modest alteration of the denotation of words. The investigation of the evolution of the meaning of words over a long time is the subject of the special scientific discipline of *hermeneutics*.

Chapter 5
Language and Information

The basic elements of a natural language text are the words. The words are combined to sentences that relate words to each other and thus form a higher-level building block.

In the DIT model a word is considered to have a *meaning*, but a *basic sentence* that is constructed out of meaningful words is the smallest unit that makes *sense*.

This *sense* is the *information item* (*Itom*), the *idea*, communicated by a *basic sentence*. (If someone looks at a *word in isolation* without any accompanying gestures, the word has *meaning* but does not confer information.) Sentences are embedded in *paragraphs*. A sequence of paragraphs makes a *story*.

The field of *Information Extraction* deals with the automatic extraction of the *Itoms*, (i.e., structured information items) that are contained in an unstructured natural language text, such as a story [38]. The *sense of a sentence* in the middle of a story is influenced by its *left context* (i.e., the context established by the previous sentences) and influences its *right context* (i.e., the context after the sentence). In natural language understanding and natural language processing the *left context* and the *right context* of a given sentence are analyzed in order to get a better recognition of the meaning of the words in the sentence and the *sense* of the given sentence [39].

In our analysis of language, we start with the *meaning of a word*.

5.1 Meaning of a Word

In order to gain an understanding of a *natural language word* we must first identify the *signifier*, i.e., the unique appearance of the word in the given *outer context*, and then grasp the *signified*, i.e., the *meaning (embodied in a concept)* that is associated with the word in the *inner context* of the hearer. A word is only understood by a

© The Author(s), under exclusive license to Springer Nature Switzerland AG 2022
H. Kopetz, *Data, Information, and Time*, SpringerBriefs in Computer Science,
https://doi.org/10.1007/978-3-030-96329-3_5

human—and thus becomes a meaningful data item—if the link between the *signifier* and the *signified* is available in the *conceptual landscape* of the hearer.

In the physical world, the signifier of a word is represented by a physical pattern, either a characteristic sound stream (in oral communication) or a sequence of scribbles (letters) in the chosen language (in written communication). A physical pattern is an unrandom discrete or continuous arrangement of *signs* either in the domain of time (such as the *audio data* above) or in the domain of physical space (such as a written word or a picture on a piece of paper, or a set of gestures). If—in oral communication—a person does not know the characteristic sound stream (e.g., a word spoken in a foreign language) or cannot recognize the characteristic features in the sound stream (due to hearing impairments), then the sound stream has no meaning to the hearer.

Let us illustrate the difference between our use of the terms *physical pattern* and meaningful *data item* by elaborating on the well-known Rosetta Stone. When the old Egyptian Rosetta Stone with its obscure patterns (the hieroglyphic inscriptions) was discovered in 1799, the meaning of the patterns could not be explained, at least not by the scientists who found the stone. It took about 20 years until the *meaning* of the patterns carved in the stone was unveiled. At this instant, the hieroglyphs became the *signifiers of symbols* that disclosed *meaning* to the human scientist.

If the characteristic features of the sound stream are perceived and are familiar to the hearer, then the link to an established concept in the conceptual landscape of the hearer is provided by an autonomous neural process of the human mind.

In the DIT model a *data item* is a symbol that consists of a *signifier* and a *signified*. The *signifier*—the name of the symbol—is the physical pattern that represents the data item in the physical world. In human communication the signifier is a *word* and the *signified* of this symbol is the *meaning of the word*, determined by the assigned concept in the mind of an attentive human receiver.

This brings us to the important issue of how the meaning of a word is established, i.e., how concepts are formed and how the link between a word and the associated concept (the *signifier* and the assigned *signified*) is established in the human mind in the first place.

According to *embodied cognition* [62] a human develops a *basic concept* and therewith assigns *meaning* to the sounds of the *identifying word* at a *basic level* when a plethora of bodily sensations (visual, acoustic, haptic, smell, taste) of a thing are perceived during a purposeful process. These sensations establish a multitude of explicit and tacit links to already existing concepts (that may not yet have a name at this early stage of language acquisition). For example, in the course of *language acquisition* a baby associates the perceived sensual impressions of a *pacifier* with the sound of the spoken word *"pacifier,"* and thus establishes the link between the spoken word and the concept. By pointing to a tree and saying *"this is a tree"* the link between the visual impression of a *tree* and the sounds of the word *"tree"* is established. After a set of basic concepts has been formed in this way, the acquired language words can be used to describe the meaning of new words and thus form more advanced concepts.

Whenever we try to achieve a goal by the execution of motor actions and experience sensory inputs (visual, acoustic, haptic, etc.) in the course of this process we are on the route to acquiring a new meaningful concept. *"Words become meaningful when a certain kind of intentionality is imposed among them"* [62, p. 180]. For example, the command *"kick the ball"* initiates a number of subconscious neural processes that control the muscles that must be activated in order to reach the given goal.

Many of the words that are used in everyday language are either a name of a *category,* a name of a *relation,* or a *proper name* of an entity. A *proper name* identifies an entity uniquely in the CSTD. The entities of a higher-level category can be things or lower-level categories, leading to an *abstraction hierarchy* [40], where the higher levels of abstraction leave out many of the detailed properties of the entities that are part of the lower-level abstractions and finally of the things that are encountered in reality.

Abstraction and categorization are essential for building general mental models that support human thinking and purposeful actions. On the other side, the links to the concrete objects in reality that have been formed at the basic level of language acquisition should not be abandoned. *"It is obvious, then, that interesting speech and writing, as well as clear thinking and psychological well-being, require the constant interplay of higher level and lower level abstractions, and the constant interplay of the verbal levels with the non-verbal ('object') level [40, p.95]."*

Humans have the important capability to identify the general structure of a mental model of a given concrete phenomenon and transfer this structure metaphorically to other phenomena. The metaphorical transposition of words and insights gained in one domain to a completely different domain is a cornerstone of human language and creativity. Take, for example, the metaphorical treatment of *time* as a moneylike resource. Time can be *saved, lost, spent, wasted,* etc. [41, p. 209].

An example for the transposition of a concrete concept to an abstract domain is the concept of a *path.* In its concrete form, a *path* means that a physical goal is reached by following an ordered sequence of physical steps from a physical starting point to the physical goal, e.g., a baby is crawling to grasp a toy or a person is hiking to the top of a mountain. This concrete concept of a path that has become meaningful at the physical (basic) level is then taken up metaphorically in a more abstract domain to describe the abstract concept of an *ordered pair* in mathematics [42, p. 141].

Stevan Harnad offers the following example to explain another methodology of advanced concept formation [31, p. 343]: Suppose the words *"horse"* and *"stripes"* are grounded at the basic level by the human senses. Then a category called *"zebra"* can be constructed by

$$"zebra" = "horse" \& "stripes",$$

where the symbols "=" and "&" are *literals.* The concept named *"zebra"* exhibits the properties of the elementary concepts *"horse"* and *"stripes."* The names of *basic concepts* are grounded in the invariant features of the sensual experience of the physical thing in the observable environment.

In the past 400 years humans have developed many instruments to expand the capability of our senses and extend the observable environment: *precise clocks* have been built to better measure the progression of time, *telescopes* have been invented to increase the scope of our vision systems, and sophisticated devices, such as a *Geiger counter,* have been developed for measuring ionizing radiation that is not directly detectable by the human senses. This enlargement of our conceptual landscape, caused by the application of sophisticated instruments, required the formation of new concepts, such as, e.g., the concept of *radioactivity,* and their relations to already existing concepts.

For a detailed discussion about the relation between body and mind, the formation of concepts and the grounding of words see [31, 41, 43, 62].

5.2 Basic Sentence

Let us look at the grammatical structure of the following basic English sentence:

$$\langle\text{subject}\rangle \quad \langle\text{predicate}\rangle \quad \langle\text{object}\rangle$$
$$\text{Tom} \quad\quad \text{possesses} \quad \text{a valid passport}$$

Figure 5.1 depicts this basic sentence in the form of a *simple knowledge* graph (see also Sect. 7.2). This simple knowledge graph provides a graphical representation of the named relation between the two entities, *subject* and *object*, of the basic sentence.

In this basic sentence the *<subject>* is a *word or phrase* denoting the proper name of a *person* (i.e., an entity), the *<predicate>* is a *word or phrase* that denotes a *relation*, and the *<object>* is a phrase that refines the specification of the relation. We call such a basic sentence consisting of the concatenation of signifiers a *proposition*, because we don't know if the *truth-value* of this sentence corresponds to the *way things actually are in reality* (correspondence theory of truth). *"The basic idea of the correspondence theory is that what we believe or say is true if it corresponds to the way things actually are—to the facts"* [44]. In the DIT model, *a verified proposition* is called a *statement*.

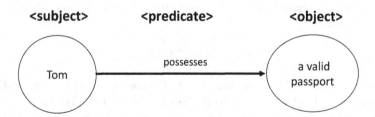

Fig. 5.1 Simple *knowledge graph* of a basic sentence

A basic sentence is called a *property sentence* if the *subject* is a thing or a construct (e.g., a *category*), the *predicate* denotes a *(possibly timed) property*, and the *object* contains the detailed characterization of the property. The detailed characterization of the property can be a *value*, either a *numerical value* expressing the magnitude of the property in agreed measurement units or an *element of an enumeration set*, such as the set of distinguished colors (see also Sect. 3.2).

The *predicate* of a basic sentence is a *verb* or a *verb phrase* that indicates the *tense*. The tense determines to what *instant* or *duration* on the timeline the predicate refers to (in German a *verb* is called a *Zeitwort*). John Lyon says about *tense* [14, p. 682]: *"The crucial fact about tense, whether we talk about sentences or propositions, is that it is a deictic category. A tensed proposition, therefore, will be, not merely time-bound, or even temporally restricted: it will contain a reference to some point or period of time which cannot be identified except in terms of the zero-point of the utterance."*

The above sentence *"Tom possesses a valid passport,"* expressed in the present tense, is *semantically meaningful*. In order to make this sentence *denotationally meaningful* we have to find the *instant* (the *zero point*) *when* the sentence has been uttered. *The* function *GPST (now)* provides the *timestamp of* the current *utterance event* of this sentence in UTC time format. By adding this contextually derived zero point to the sentence, the instant of utterance is fixed on the timeline and the sentence becomes *denotationally meaningful* [27, p. 221].

If the *zero point* of the sentence *"Tom possesses a valid passport"* lies within the *validity interval* that is contained in the passport then this sentence is *true*. Let us now assume that this sentence is written on a piece of paper and seen by a reader at some later time. If the zero point of the *reading event* is outside the *validity interval* that is contained in the passport, then the sentence (which is expressed in the *present tense*) is *false*. The flow of time has changed the *truth-value* of this *semantically meaningful* sentence.

Since the UTC time of *now* is provided by the function GPST(now), it is possible to determine whether the zero point of an utterance (which is often the present point in time) lies within the temporal interval that is associated with the predicate of the proposition.

The truth-value of a proposition can change as time progresses. Consider the example of a traffic light, which changes periodically—as time flows—between the states *red*, *yellow*, and *green*. The proposition *the traffic light is green* is only true if the zero point of this utterance lies in an interval of the timeline where the traffic light is green.

There are thus actually two references to time in a basic sentence, the *tense* of the predicate and the *zero point of the utterance*.

If we look at a typical basic sentence from the aspect of timing, in the majority of cases the temporal aspect of a proposition is communicated, in addition to the point of utterance, by the *predicate*, the Zeitwort. Compared to the *predicate*, the meaning of the *object* and the *subject* does not convey knowledge about the temporal aspect—most often they are *static* in the CSTD. It is the relation between *object* and *subject*, the predicate of a basic sentence, that informs about the timing. For this reason, we decided to add the temporal parameters of a basic sentence that determine at what sections of the timeline the temporal validity of the proposition holds, to the predicate in the DIT model.

Let us now look at the three *property sentences, illustrated by the knowledge graph* of Fig. 5.2 and uttered today, on 2021 08 03.

Sentence 1a *"Tom has a passport which is valid between the timestamps 2015 07 03 and 2025 07 02"* is *true* if the *instant of reading* the sentence (the *zero point*) is within the cited *validity interval* that is limited by the two timestamps contained in the passport. These two timestamps limit the validity interval of the passport.

Sentence 1b *"Tom has a weight of* 101 kg" is *true* at the time of measurement contained in the predicate. If we refer to this measurement sometimes later, the weight might have changed. An upper bound of this *change error* can be established if the *maximum gradient* of the weight change and the duration of the interval since the last measurement are known. If we accept a bounded measurement error and know the dynamics of a process, we can calculate a second timestamp that limits the validity interval for the use of this measurement. This technique is widely deployed to establish the sampling rate in a real-time control system [28, p. 7].

Sentence 1c reports about an event, where the past timestamp of occurrence of the event is contained in the predicate.

Note that all fields of the three propositions of Fig. 5.2 are grounded in reality provided that the reader is aware of the *zero point of the utterance* and knows *Tom*, what is a *passport*, what is a *timestamp*, and what is the meaning of the cited words, such as *weight, involve, car accident,* etc.

A proposition is only meaningful to a human if all words of the proposition are grounded in in the mind of the human.

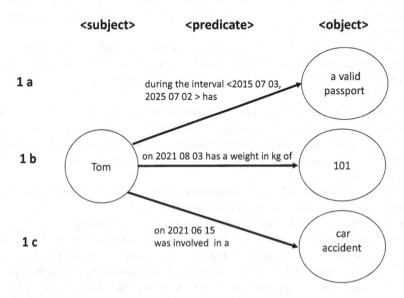

Fig. 5.2 Knowledge graph of three property sentences

5.3 Temporal Validity Function

In Sect. 3.1 we introduced two basic concepts to denote the position of a happening on the absolute timeline: an *event* that occurs at an *instant* (a cut of the timeline) and is characterized by a single timestamp and a *state* or *process* that is *active* during an *interval* (a section of the timeline) and can be characterized by two timestamps, one for the start and one for the termination of the interval.

If the predicate of a sentence informs about a past event, then the timestamp of the occurrence of the event provides the required temporal information. However, a tensed natural language provides many more linguistic structures to denote the sections of the timeline when a predicate of a basic sentence is meant to hold. The specification of a happening on the timeline can be relative to an earlier or later happening or it can contain an absolute future timestamp, as shown in the following examples:

⟨subject⟩	⟨predicate⟩	⟨object⟩
⟨Tom⟩	⟨will enter ten minutes before the lectures starts⟩	⟨the school building⟩
	or	
⟨Tom⟩	⟨will leave ten minutes after the lectures terminates⟩	⟨the school building⟩
	or	
⟨Tom⟩	⟨enters at 21 11 18 08 30⟩	⟨the school building⟩

In the DIT model we introduce the concept of a *temporal validity function* (*TVF*) to provide the means to express some of the more involved temporal relations that are communicated in a natural language sentence about a particular scenario.

In its basic form, the TVF has two input parameters: the *<scenario_name>* that is the name of the scenario that is referred to in a sentence, and a *<timestamp>*. The *temporal validity function* TVF(*<scenario_name>*,*<timestamp>*) delivers the logical value TRUE if the timestamp lies within a *validity section* of the timeline, i.e., a section when the predicate of the proposition expressed in the tensed natural language sentence about the scenario is meant to hold. If this is the case then

$$\text{TVF}\big(\langle scenario\_name\rangle, \langle \text{timestamp}\rangle\big)$$

is *TRUE*, otherwise it is FALSE.

Let us look at the following simple example of the opening hours of MYBARBER:

Day of the week	Opens	Closes
Monday	1:00 p.m.	5:00 p.m.
Tuesday	9:00 a.m.	5:00 p.m.
Wednesday	9:00 a.m.	5:00 p.m.
Thursday	9:00 a.m.	5:00 p.m.
Friday	9:00 a.m.	5:00 p.m.
Saturday	9:00 a.m.	1:00 p.m.
Sunday	Closed	

A graphical representation of the validity sections specified by this table is shown in Fig. 5.3.

If a person would like to know if MYBARBER is *now* open she/he can ask.

$$TVF\big(MYBARBER, \ GPST\big(now\big)\big) = ?$$

and she/he will get as an answer either *TRUE* (if MYBARBER is open) or FALSE (if MYBARBER is not open). This question can be repeated for any instant in the future or the past to learn whether MYBARBER is *open* at that instant.

5.4   Information Item—Itom

In the DIT model we call the *sense*, i.e., the *denotational meaning of a proposition* an *information item*, abbreviated by *Itom* [30, p. 19]. To arrive at the *sense of a proposition* (the Itom) we require a semantically meaningful proposition (i.e., a proposition composed of meaningful words) augmented with temporal parameters that indicate the validity interval of the scenario (e.g., a TVF function) and the *zero point* (or any desired instant) when the proposition is *questioned to hold*.

An *Itom* (information item) represents *an idea in the form of a timed understandable proposition*. **The temporal properties of the predicate of the proposition must be communicated in the proposition, either directly or by context. In the DIT model we say** *words* **have** *meaning*, **but an** *Itom* **makes** *sense*.

An *idea* is "*any conception existing in the mind as a result of mental understanding, awareness, or activity*" [dictionary.com] or "*an understanding, thought or*

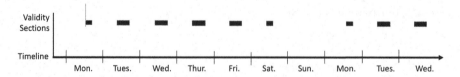

Fig. 5.3 Validity sections on the timeline

picture in your mind" [Cambridge Dictionary]. The notion of *understandability* assumes the presence of a conscious human with an attentive mind who can explain the meaning of the words used in the proposition and thus has the capability to grasp the sense of an Itom.

An *Itom* expresses a *named link* between two meaningful words that denote established concepts. This link must contain temporal parameters *(e.g., a TVF function)* to indicate the time when this link is assumed to hold. An Itom can be expressed in many different forms (e.g., with different words in a given language or in different languages).

The *sense* of an *Itom* must remain the same if the representation is changed from one form to another form.

Let us now look at some of the important characteristics of an *Itom* in the DIT model [30, p. 22]:

- **Truthfulness:** Our conception of an Itom does not make any assumptions whether the information carried by an Itom is *true* (correspondence theory of truth), *misinformation* (accidentally false), or *disinformation* (intentionally false—fake news). It is often the case that only sometime after an Itom has appeared that it can be decided whether the information contained in the Itom is *true* or *false.*
- **Newness:** The aspect of *newness of information* to the receiver and associated metrics about the subjective value or the subjective utility of the Itom to a receiver are not part of the DIT model. We feel that it is not possible to capture *the totality of knowledge* that is contained in the personal knowledge base—the *conceptual landscape*—of a human. This is necessary if we want to determine whether the information contained in an Itom is new with respect to this knowledge base.
- **Temporal Aspects:** The sense of an atomic sentence in the physical world—*the Itom*—is most often time-dependent. The Itom must inform when the predicate of the proposition holds (e.g., by reference to a TVF function).
- **Relativity:** While the Itom itself does not depend on any particular representation, any representation of an Itom, i.e., the appearance of the Itom in the physical world (the *chosen signifiers*) must consider the context that is shared among the group of people who is expected to deal with the Itom. We call this group of people that is expected to interact with the Itom the *clientele of the Itom*. Since there exists no absolute context, there cannot be an absolute representation of an Itom.

If we envision the conceptual landscape as a large knowledge graph where concepts are linked by named and timed connections, then an Itom that is new to a receiver establishes a new link in this knowledge graph (see Sect. 7.2).

This picture of the conceptual landscape as a huge knowledge graph has some similarity to the physical connections among neurons in the human brain where *trillions of synapsis* establish the links among the *billions of neurons* in the cerebral cortex.

Chapter 6
Data in Communication

6.1 Communication Among Humans

The *Merriam Webster* dictionary defines communication as follows:

- *A process by which information is exchanged between individuals through a common system of symbols, signs or behavior;*
- *the function of pheromones in insect communication.*

Since *information* consists of one or more *Itoms*, the first part of this definition can be viewed as a process where Itoms are exchanged between humans. We cover the second part of this definition—the *function of pheromones*—in the section on *Stigmergic Communication*.

Oral Communication What are the steps that take place when an *Itom* is transmitted in oral communication from one human (the sender) to another human (the receiver)? As mentioned before, an Itom in the mind of the sender contains an idea in the form of an *understandable proposition* that deals with a *timed property of a scenario*.

The first step in the transmission of an Itom involves a decision about the external representation of the Itom in the mind of the sender. Many details have to be settled when creating the external representation of an Itom, e.g., the choice of a set of symbols (a specific language), the picking of the symbols (the words in the language), the place and time where and when the communication act takes place, etc. The same semantic content—the *sense* of an Itom—can be represented by very different representations in the physical environment.

We partition the totality of all details of a representation of an Itom in the physical world into two disjoint sets: the *shared details* (those details common to the *inner context* of the sender and receiver, called the *shared inner context*)

H. Kopetz, *Data, Information, and Time*, SpringerBriefs in Computer Science, https://doi.org/10.1007/978-3-030-96329-3_6

and the *particular details* (those details that are not part of the *shared inner context*).

Only the *particular details* of an Itom must be transmitted in a communication act from the sender to the receiver in order that the receiver can recover the *sense* of the Itom from the received signifiers. Let us assume that the *particular details* of an idea that are expressed by the Itom are available in the mind of the sender in the form of a sequence of words in the chosen language. The dynamic core of the speaker sends these words via an output port to the autonomous neural circuitry that generates a sequence of phonemes and produces detailed motor outputs to the muscles of the larynx. The larynx delivers the intended sound pattern—a *stream of sounds*—to the physical environment. The sender can modulate the stream of sounds to provide special emphasis to sections of speech. We call this stream of sounds the *audio data* of the sender. In a successful oral communication act the audio data that is produced by the sender arrives at the ear of the receiver and is transformed by autonomous neural processes in the ear and in the brain of the receiver such that the intended words are available at an input port of the dynamic core of the receiver. The receiver decodes the meaning of the words by accessing his linguistic memory that assigns meaning to words.

We call a sequence of words that represents a single Itom and is presented in the physical world as a single stream of sounds a *simple message*. A *message* is the concatenation of one or more simple messages that is transmitted as a unit.

It is important to distinguish oral communication in a dialogue among a group of people from oral communication when delivering a speech to a large audience. In a dialogue, the questions and answers, framed in messages, of the dialogue partners help to align the *inner contexts* of the partners. When delivering a speech, a speaker publishes his thoughts in one single stroke in a *grand message* without the possibility to get detailed feedback from the audience, i.e., the *clientele of the Itoms*. The speaker must align his/her inner context with the assumed outer context of the audience and hope that a sufficiently good alignment between this assumed outer context of the audience and the inner contexts of the persons in the audience is present.

Written Communication In written communication the sender augments the sequence of words that are formed in his/her mind with punctuation marks (e.g., spaces, commas, etc.) to delineate the syntactic units of the language and sends this augmented sequence of words via an output port of the dynamic core to the autonomous neural circuitry that controls the motor commands for writing this sequence of words on a physical medium, e.g., a piece of paper or the keyboard of a computer. At this instant, the words that originated in the human mind of the sender are embodied as a sequence of an observable pattern, the signifiers, in the physical world. These physical patterns, the signifiers of data items, can be accessed by the receiver at some later time. A human receiver reads the written words and arrives at the meaning of the words in his mind by using his linguistic memory and his inner context at the instant of reading the words.

One main difference between written communication and oral communication is the timing. While in oral communication the production of speech is synchronized

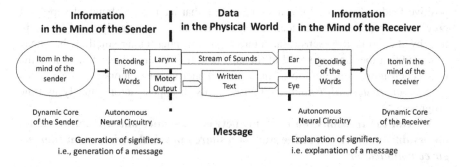

Fig. 6.1 The DIT model of human communication by the use of language

with the analysis of the speech by the receiver, there can be an arbitrary time delay between the writing of a text and the reading of a text. In a dynamic scenario, the truth-value of an Itom that reports about a dynamic property of the world at the instant of writing may differ from the truth-value of this Itom at the instant of reading.

The change of the truth-value of an Itom by the progression of real time is of utmost concern in the design of a real-time control system. In a real-time system, a *validity interval* must be assigned to every observation of a dynamic entity. The observed value is only allowed to be used within this validity interval. Take as an example the Itom: *the traffic light is green*. If this Itom is used outside the validity interval—at an instant when the traffic light has already changed to *red*—then an accident may occur [Kop12, p. 4].

Figure 6.1 summarizes the DIT model for the information transfer of an Itom, i.e., an idea, by the use of language from the mind of a human sender via different physical data channels to the mind of a human receiver. On the left side of Fig. 6.1 we see the processes that take place in the mind of the sender where the signifiers are generated for a symbol-based data transmission. In the physical word, the Itoms appear in the form of a *message* that transports the signifiers of the data items. The complementary process of data explanation between the start of sensing the message and the delivery of the message to the input port of the dynamic core of the receiver is depicted on the right side. In Fig. 6.1 we depict two different physical channels, an acoustic channel to transmit audio data and a text channel to transmit written text.

6.2 Stigmergic Communication

The term *stigmergy* was coined by the biologist Grasse [45] to describe the communication among ants when they look for prey. Whenever an ant builds or follows a trail, it deposits a greater or lesser amount of the whiffing chemical pheromone on the trail, depending on whether it has successfully found a prey or not. Due to positive feedback successful trails—i.e., trails that lead to an abundant supply of prey—end up with a high concentration of pheromone. The nearly blind ants capture by their olfactory sense the intensity of the pheromone smell. It has been observed that the running speed of the ants on a trail is a nonlinear function of the trail's pheromone concentration. Since the trail pheromone evaporates—we call this process *environmental dynamics*—unused trails disappear autonomously as time progresses.

We call the transmission of Itoms between a sender and a receiver via an observable modification of the state of a shared physical environment *stigmergic communication.*

In contrast to the transmission of signifiers of symbols—we call this *symbol-based communication*, the *stigmergic communication* does not require the use of symbols. *Stigmergic communication* between one or more senders and one or more receivers is realized in the following steps:

1. A sender sends a motor command to an actuator that alters the state of the physical environment.
2. This altered state of the physical environment is possibly modified by *environmental dynamics* resulting in a *modified altered state*.
3. A sensor of the receiver observes this modified altered state and produces a sense data item that is preprocessed and sent to the dynamic core of the receiver.
4. The sense data item is combined with the information retrieved from the inner context of the receiver to generate one or more Itoms.

The indirect communication among the drivers of cars at a busy intersection is a good example for *stigmergic communication*. Although the drivers can come from different backgrounds and have limited shared *inner context* in their conceptual landscapes (e.g., they don't even speak the same language) they communicate by observing the changes in the state of the environment caused by the actions of the other drivers on the road.

Whereas human communication by the use of language is intentional, stigmergic communication can happen with or without any explicit intention of the sender.

Figure 6.2 depicts the information flow from a human sender to a human receiver via a stigmergic communication channel that can be disturbed by environmental dynamics.

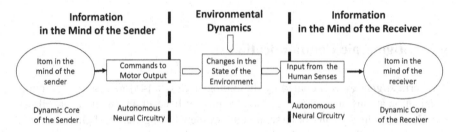

Fig. 6.2 The DIT model of human communication by the use of stigmergic communication

Sign language of the deaf and dump people is similar to conventional language used in oral communication, but uses a different representation (physical gestures) to communicate the words of a proposition.

6.3 Data in Cyberspace

In a computer program the *signifier* of a *data item* is a *token name* (e.g., the name of a *variable* in a program) or a *literal*. The *signified* of a token name is a *token*. A *token is a meaningless placeholder* from the world of *constructs* that can house a *dynamic value* and can take part in a set of computations (see Sect. 3.3). The *signified of literal* is the *constant value* indicated by the *gestalt* of the signifier.

When considering a data item in cyberspace, the definition of the term *data item* introduced in Sect. 5.1 has to be revisited, because there is not necessarily a human with an attentive mind present during the operation of a computer system, e.g., an autonomous real-time control system. We thus extend the definition of a data item of Sect. 5.1 as follows:

In the DIT model a *data item* is a symbol that consists of a *signifier* and a *signified*. The *signifier*—the name of the symbol (e.g., a word or a variable name)— is the physical pattern that represents the data item in the physical world.

- **In human communication the *signified* of this symbol is the meaning of the data item, determined by the concept in the mind of an attentive human receiver.**
- **In a computer system the *signified* of this symbol is the *value* housed by the token that is operationally explained by the use of the variable name in the computer program (operational definition).**

In both cases a *data item* is a *whole* that consists of two parts, the *signifier* and the *signified*. If we take the whole apart and look at each part in isolation, then the notion of a *data item* breaks.

In a computer system, the *signifier* of a data item, when considered in isolation, is a meaningless pattern in the physical world. The *signified of a variable in a computer program*, considered in isolation, is a lonesome numeric or alphanumeric value or a bit pattern (e.g., picture) that is detached from its operational explanation that is provided by the computer program that uses the *variable name* in its operations.

If we consistently replace in a complete program all instances of a given token name (a variable name) by another token name (another variable name), then the computations performed with the values are not changed. Har [43, p. 379] notes: *"Computation is interpretable symbol manipulation. Symbols are objects that are manipulated on the basis of rules operating only on their shapes (i.e., the signifiers), which are arbitrary in relation to what they can be interpreted as meaning."*

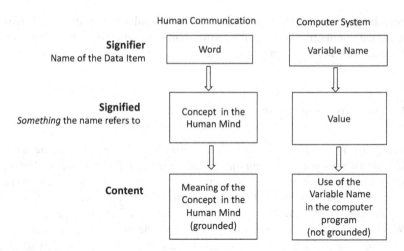

Fig. 6.3 *Signifier* and *signified* of a data item

Figure 6.3 shows the differences between the *signifier,* the *signified,* and the *meaning* of a data item in human communication and in a computer system.

If the name of a variable in a program (Fig. 6.3) is a meaningful word that denotes (as its *signified*) an established concept in the mind of a human, then the value of this *variable is grounded* and can be considered a (possibly *degenerate*) *Itom* that carries *sense*.

From the point of view of the DIT model an Itom is *degenerate* if the required temporal information is missing.

A variable of a program (with a meaningful variable name) contains the three parts *(subject, predicate,* and *object)* of a basic sentence, where every one of these three parts carries meaning. The *subject* is the concept denoted by the meaningful word that is used as a variable name. The *predicate* is implied and means that the value of the object is assigned to the subject and the *external context* determines the interpretation of the value. The object is either a (static) literal, a *constant,* that derives its static value out of its *gestalt* (a literal consisting of digits has the meaning of a numerical value) or the (dynamic) value stored in the placeholder. The sense of a meaningful variable can thus be explained as follows: *The concept denoted by the variable name is associated with the value housed in the placeholder at the instant of inspection of the variable.*

An algorithm, implemented by a program, establishes formal relations among a set of tokens. If we ground the tokens by assigning meaningful words to the tokens, then these *formal relations* model *actual relations* about the assigned concepts that are supposed to exist in reality. If these *actual relations* are *true* in reality, then we say that the program is *correct*.

Let us look at a proposition expressed in the form of an assignment statement in a programming language, to describe the cons*truct of a variable in a computer program* in more detail:

$$\langle subject \rangle \quad \langle predicate \rangle \quad \langle object \rangle$$
$$x \qquad\qquad = \qquad\qquad 101$$

The variable name x takes (at the time of execution of this statement) *the numeric value of the literal string of digits 101*. The *numeric value* of the *literal string of digits 101* depends on the *chosen notation*. In the decimal system the *string of digits 101* expresses the numeric value 101. In the binary system the numeric value of the *string of digits 101* is 5 (expressed in decimal notation). In order to get at the correct numeric value, we have to agree about the context—in this case about the base or the *data type* (decimal or binary).

But even if we agree that the digits 101 have the numeric value of 101 this proposition has no meaning in the real world since not all fields of the proposition are grounded. It is not known what is the meaning of the variable x (a token name), nor when the predicate of the statement is executed, nor what measurement units are the basis of the numeric value 101. In the DIT model we say that the *variable x* and the *meaning of the numeric value 101* are *ungrounded*.

If, however, we *ground* (by considering the context) that the *variable name x* means the *weight of Tom, the weight is expressed in kg* (as implied by the external context in Europe) and the zero point of the utterance expresses the instant of measurement, then this statement makes *sense* in the real world and conveys information to a human user. (In the US the *external context* implies that the measurement units are pounds.)

Let us now look at the representation of the propositions of Fig. 5.2 within a computer program where we replace the meaningful words of Fig. 5.2 by meaningless token names in Fig. 6.4. The token names that are shown under the headings *subject, predicate,* and *object* are ungrounded, i.e., they have no meaning in reality. Inside the computer, these token names are sufficient to perform the required computations.

At the human/computer interface the token names of Fig. 6.4 must be grounded by the assignment of *meaningful words* to the tokens in order that a human user can get an *understanding* of the referenced data items:

- T1 the name of the person *Tom* that must be known to the user.
- T2 has *something* which is valid between <*two timestamps* > and is uttered at a known *zero point*.
- T3 has a weight measured in kg on the specified date.
- T4 was involved in *something* during the specified interval.
- T5 denoted a passport.
- T6 is the numeric value for the weight on the specified date.
- T7 denotes a car accident that is the object of the predicate T4.

Another way to ground the tokens is the provision of sensors such that the computer can observe the physical environment. For example, an interface of token T3 to the scale that measures the weight of Tom grounds the acquired value. This grounding of the collected data item is achieved by the design of the sensor and the

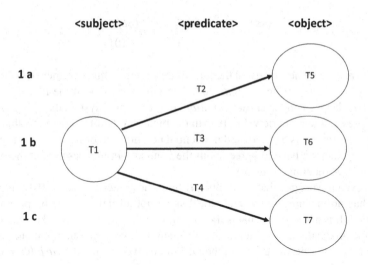

Fig. 6.4 Sentences of Fig. 5.2 stored in a computer

logic of the program, developed by a human programmer who understands the operation of the scale.

There is a fundamental difference in storing and handling of information and data between humans and computers. Humans communicate and reason about phenomena in the world by the use of *Itoms*. An *Itom* (i.e., the *sense of a proposition*) must be embedded in the contextual landscape (see Chap. 4) of the prospective human user.

Machines, designed by humans, *transfer* and process a *data item* (i.e., *a signified of a meaningless symbol name*) according to algorithms provided by human programmers. The human programmers, who develop the algorithms, must know the precise real-word meaning of the name of a data item (the signifier) that is used as input or produced as output of a computation.

Chapter 7
Data in Archival Systems

An *archive* is a repository that holds documents of *permanent historical informa-tion (a vast plurality of Itoms)* that are dated and stored on different kinds of media in order that this information can be accessed and analyzed at some future date. The documents can be kept in analogue or digital form. In a computer archive the data are stored in digital form on some protected digital storage media.

7.1 Data Structures

In a database system the *signified* (the value) of a *data item* is stored in a *data struc-ture*. A data structure provides the framework (the *database schema*) for the organi-zation, the access, and the explanation of the stored values. The database schema—the description of the framework—can provide for the *grounding* of the *value*. It depends on the concrete explanation communicated by the database schema in a particular database whether the *whole*, the value in the data structure together with the explanation provided by the database schema, carries only meaning or, most often, makes sense.

An elementary form of a data structure is a simple *file* that consists of a sequence of *records*, where every record contains a number of *data fields*. Every data field can house a *value*. A file can be depicted by a two-dimensional table that carries a name—the *file name*. The *file name* explains the general external context of the data items contained in the file in a language that is familiar to the prospective users. The file name may also provide the temporal parameters required by the DIT model. The *file name* is an integral part of the explanation that is needed to understand the *val-ues* that are contained in the file.

Every row of a two-dimensional file structure (depicted by a table) contains a record with a *record name* and every column of the table carries a *column name*. At

© The Author(s), under exclusive license to Springer Nature Switzerland AG 2022
H. Kopetz, *Data, Information, and Time*, SpringerBriefs in Computer Science,
https://doi.org/10.1007/978-3-030-96329-3_7

the intersection of the row and the column is a *value* that is explained by the *record name* and the *column name*.

A *data item* is a *signifier* that denotes a *signified*. In Sect. 3.3 we have introduced four types of *signifiers* in the DIT model

1. a proper name,
2. a token name,
3. a literal,
4. a word of a natural language.

Let us now look at the *signified* of each one of these *signifiers*. If the signifier is a *proper name* then it refers to a unique entity in the considered space-time domain (CSTD). This entity—in many cases a person—must be familiar to a prospective user of the data structure. If the signifier is a *token name* then the signified is a meaningless placeholder of a token system that can hold a value and can be related to other meaningless placeholders of the token system. The signified of a *literal*—in many cases a set of numeric symbols that denote a numeric value in the chosen numeric notation—can be derived from the gestalt of the *signifier* (the literal). This connection between the gestalt of the signifier and the meaning of the signified must be known to the prospective user, i.e., a person must know what a number signifier stands for. The signified of a *word of a natural language*—normally represented in the form of a string of characters—must be linked to a familiar concept in the mind of a person that is part of the language community. In Sect. 5.1 we have discussed the topic of *concept formation* in detail, i.e., the means by which a natural language word acquires meaning.

A *value* is located at the intersection of a row and a column of the two-dimensional table. If the *row name* and the *column name* are *grounded* (i.e., they are *meaningful* names) and the value is a *literal* then the *triple < row name, column name, value>* forms a *(possibly degenerate) Itom*.

Let us look at the simple example of a file that contains the sizes and the weights of students that are part of a school class with the class name 3A. About twice a year these measurements are taken and recorded in the archival file depicted in Fig. 7.1. In this case the *file name* contains the required temporal information.

Size and Weight of the Students in Class 3A,

measured on 2022 11 11

Name/Property	Size in cm	Weight in kg	-------------
Paul	160	61	...
Ann	155	53	...
---------	...	...	...

Fig. 7.1 Tabular form of data

All signifiers that appear in this file are meaningful. The file name—*Size and Weight of the Students in Class 3A, measured on 2022 11 11*—informs about the context of the file and contains the required temporal parameters. A reader of the table must be familiar with the words used in the title and must know that class 3A is part of a particular school. The name 3A refines the external context of this file.

The first column contains the proper names of the students that are members of class 3A. The identified students are unique and known to the teacher. The header of the second column informs the reader that the displayed values denote the size of a student measured in cm. The header of the third column informs the reader that the displayed values denote the weight of a student measured in kg. The entries at the intersection of the row name and column name are literals that denote a numeric value of the measurements in the decimal notation.

The *information* contained in the file of Fig. 7.1 can be expressed by the following six Itoms:

1. *On 2021 11 11 Paul has a size of 160 cm.*
2. *On 2021 11 11 Ann has a size of 155 cm.*
3. *On 2021 11 11 Paul weighs 61 kg.*
4. *On 2021 11 11 Ann weighs 53 kg.*
5. *On 2021 11 11 Paul belongs to Class 3A.*
6. *On 2021 11 11 Ann belongs to Class 3A.*

The first four of these Itoms refer to the data fields of the table of Fig. 7.1. The last two Itoms are derived from the fact that Paul and Ann appear in the table, i.e., they are members of class 3A that is identified in the file name.

These six Itoms that are listed above can be presented in the form of very different tabular data structures. For example, we can provide a set of separate files, each one with the size and weight of a student of class 3A, as a function of time (Fig. 7.2). In this table, the proper name of the student appears in the file name. The dates of measurement form the column names contained in row one. Rows two and three of Fig. 7.2 shows a *time series of values*, where a row contains the values of a property as a function of time. The table of Fig. 7.2 holds additional values that inform the reader about the classes Paul has been attending in the previous school year.

If we choose the data structure of Fig. 7.1, we require a separate file for every *date of measurement*. If we choose the data structure of Fig. 7.2, we require a

Size and Weight of Paul

Property/Date	2020 11 10	2021 05 08	2021 11 11
Size in cm	153	157	160
Weight in kg	58	60	61
Member of Class	2B	2B	3A

Fig. 7.2 Time series of data of Fig. 7.1

separate file for *every student*. We call the totality of all related files that contain the values of a selected phenomenon, irrespective of the organization of the data, a *DIT-database*. A *DIT-database* thus comprises a (possibly very large) plurality of database tables.

In some archival systems the values and the database schema and the values are stored on different media. The meaning of a data item can only be properly retrieved from the archived values if the data access programs (that contain the database schema and provide the explanation of the values) and the values are compatible. If, in the course of time, new versions of the programs are developed that are incompatible with the structure of the stored values, then it is not possible to retrieve the meaning out of the stored values anymore.

7.2   Knowledge Graphs

The term *knowledge graph* was coined in 1972 by E. Schneider [46] during the design of *semantic networks* for a modular instructional course system. A semantic network is a graph structure which represents a concept as a node and a semantic relation between concepts as a link. In semantic network terminology a *simple semantic graph* consists of two nodes and a link between these two nodes. A *simple semantic graph* is sometimes called a *fact*. For a deep discussion on the notions of *knowledge* and *fact* see ref. [47].

On May 16, 2012—40 years later—Google presented the *Google Knowledge Graph* as a way to significantly enhance the value of information returned by Google searches [48]: *"The Knowledge Graph enables you to search for things, people or places that Google knows about—landmarks, celebrities, cities, sports teams, buildings, geographical features, movies, celestial objects, works of art and more—and instantly get information that's relevant to your query. This is a critical first step towards building the next generation of search, which taps into the collective intelligence of the web and understands the world a bit more like people do."* The size of the Google Knowledge Graph grew tremendously since its introduction in 2012. Google reported in May 2020 [49] that the Google Knowledge Graph contained 500 billion facts and about five billion entities.

Since the publication of the Google Knowledge Graph in 2012, the notion of a *knowledge graph* is widely discussed in the literature, albeit with differing connotations [50]. In the DIT model a *knowledge graph* is a graphical structure that depicts the entities of the considered space-time domain (CSTD) as nodes and a relationship among entities as links between related nodes. In a *DIT knowledge* graph all entities and links must be grounded by naming them with meaningful words and the links must be annotated with temporal parameters to denote when the link is temporally valid on the timeline. If the link is valid during the whole CSTD, then the temporal parameters may be omitted.

Let us represent the six Itoms of Sect. 7.1 that are contained in Fig. 7.1 by a DIT knowledge graph (Fig. 7.3).

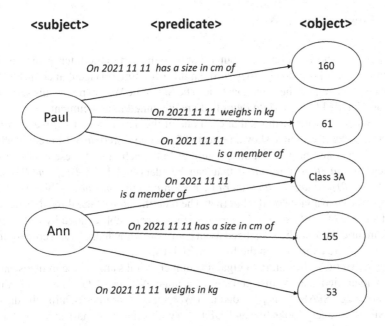

Fig. 7.3 Knowledge graph of the table in Fig. 7.1

In this knowledge graph (Fig. 7.3) every one of the six Itoms of Sect. 7.1 is depicted as a single link between two nodes. In the DIT model we call a single link and the two nodes that are connected by this link a *primitive* of the DIT knowledge graph. If the link does not hold in the whole CSTD, then this link must be annotated with temporal parameters that specify the temporal validity interval of the link.

An *Itom* is a *primitive* of a DIT knowledge graph.

The term *fact* that is used in the context of semantic networks and the Google Knowledge Graph is related to our term *Itom*. The fundamental differences between these two terms are in the *truth value* and the *handling of time*. An *Itom* must contain, as part of its predicate, a specification when the Itom is *valid* on the timeline. In the DIT model even a *temporally valid Itom* does not necessarily have to be TRUE. In the Google Knowledge Graph, it is normally assumed that a *fact* is TRUE. A consequent annotation of the Google Knowledge Graph with temporal parameters makes it possible to check by a computer program whether the "*information that's relevant to your query*" is temporally consistent and temporally valid (see the above quotation from the Google Knowledge Graph). A good survey about the work on temporal knowledge graphs is provided by Kaz [51].

Can we envision that all Itoms of the *conceptual landscape* in the mind of a human can be depicted as a *huge DIT knowledge graph*? At the moment, **the answer is definitely no,** because a plethora of the Itoms in the conceptual landscape of a human is tacit and not accessible to the dynamic core that is the neural correlate of consciousness. Since we are not aware of our tacit knowledge we cannot communicate this knowledge to the outside world.

7.3   The Semantic Web

Most persons who work on a computer that is connected to the Internet are familiar with the services provided by *hypertext*, an infrastructure service that connects documents that are not on the same machine. The Semantic Web expands this service to the more detailed level of *data items* that are contained in a document.

The Semantic Web assumes that each one of the data items of a *three data item statement* (a basic sentence shown in Sect. 3.2) can be stored on a different machine on the Internet and provides a unique reference to each one of these data items. It calls each *data item* a *resource* that can be identified by a *Uniform Resource Identifier (URI)—a unique identifier of a resource on the Internet—*which is a basic naming service available on the Internet. The identification of the three data items is called a *triple* of the *Resource Description Framework,* abbreviated by *RDF triple.* The Semantic Web can be visualized as an enormous knowledge graph composed of the facts that are expressed in the form of RDF triples.

The Semantic Web contains a gigantic number of links among the immense numbers of identified data items, generating a huge Web of Data. The standardized query language SPARQL is provided as a Web service for interrogating the data.

A SPARQL query looks like an RDF triple with a question mark standing for the requested data item:

$$\mathbf{Ask} : \langle \text{Paul} \rangle \langle \text{has a weight measured in kg} \rangle \langle ? \rangle$$
$$\mathbf{Answer} : 101$$

Inside the semantic web, the many data items that are stored in the web are related to each other, but neither the data items nor the relations are necessarily grounded in reality. The assignment of grounded words to the data items at the Human-Computer Interface grounds the data items in the language of the user such that semantically meaningful propositions that deliver Itoms are provided to the human user.

Both the *RDF triple* and the *Itom* orient themselves on the basic structure of an English sentence: *<subject> <predicate> <object>*. The main differences between an *RDF triple* and an *Itom* are:

- **Grounding of symbols**: Inside the computer *RDF triples* can use *token names* that are *ungrounded in reality* but are formally related to other *token names*. At a human-computer interface, the signifiers used to name a token or a relation should be meaningful *natural language words* that are grounded in the mind of the prospective human user.
- **Relation among entities**: The relations among the symbols of *Itoms* in the human mind are partly *rational* and partly *unconscious*. The many unconscious relations, some of them metaphorical, play an important role in human creativity. In the semantic web the relations among the entities must be provided explicitly by the human RDF programmer.

- **Handling of time**: Itoms contain temporal parameters to place the Itom in the timeline.

  The semantic net contains no special syntactic provisions to deal with the temporal context of an RDF triple. However, temporal extensions of RDF graphs have been widely studied [63].

7.4 Big Data Analytics

The exponential decline in the cost of digital computers over the past 50 years (a consequence of Moore's law) has made it economically feasible to automate many operational processes in an enterprise. The digitalization of routine operating procedures generates, as a side effect, a large number of *archival data items* about the activities that are carried out in these diverse operational processes. The analysis of this enormous database can bring to light many hidden dependencies and correlations that are contained in this huge database and are of great value for the strategic decisions of management.

By linking the data items that are collected in different operational processes we generate Itoms, i.e., information.

Let us look at the example of the course of the digitalization of a *retail shop* starting from the *old times*—when no computers were available—up to today's highly integrated big databases.

In the *old times* the owner of a typical retail shop typed the cost of the items purchased by a customer into a mechanical cash register, figured out the total and collected the indicated sum from the customer *in cash*. With the widespread use of EAN codes attached to items and the introduction of computer-based cash registers, the EAN code of a purchased item is scanned by the cashier, the price of the item is retrieved from a database, and the total is collected from the customer. As a side effect, a time-stamped sales record for every sold item is generated and the logistics database is updated. In the next phase, the customer paid by credit card and the name of the customer is added to a purchased item. The retail shop is acquired by a supermarket chain that also operates pharmacies and collects the data about the medications bought by a customer. It is now possible to link the food purchased with the medication bought by a customer. This *internal data*—the data that are collected within an organization—can be augmented by *external data*, i.e., data about conditions and events external to the organization, such as weather conditions, catastrophic events such as a power outage, political decision, etc. In such a system every day millions of records are generated and *a big database* containing terabytes of data is developed over time—giving rise to the term *big data*.

This huge database contains many hidden facts about the functioning of the organization, the behavior of customers, and the development of markets as a consequence of changes in the environment. The significant drop in the cost of data storage and data processing has made it possible to analyze such a huge database by advanced statistic and AI methods to uncover the correlations and dependencies that are hidden within this database.

Russom [52] characterizes *big data* by three properties: *data size*, *data variety*, and *data velocity*. In addition to the *size* of the database (which has been discussed above) the *variety of data* refers to the different representations of the data. In addition to digitized data, *analogue data* in the form of pictures and spoken language can be added to the database. Nowadays there are *machine learning tools* available to extract out of the analogue data some of the characteristic features that are of interest. *Data velocity* refers to the time lag between the collection of the data and the analysis of the data. For example, the consequences of a catastrophic event that affects the exchange rate of currencies should be available within a short time in order that a timely reaction by the financial department of an enterprise can be initiated.

Imagine the visualization of this huge database in the form of a *knowledge graph*. Such a knowledge graph contains many millions of nodes and edges. Remember that every subgraph of this knowledge graph (that consists of two nodes, the *object* and *subject* that are connected by a link, the *predicate*) represents an *information item*, i.e., *Itom*. In the DIT model the temporal parameters of the Itom are part of the *predicate*. If the predicate informs about an *event*, then the timestamp of the occurrence of the event must be recorded. If the predicate informs about *state*, then two timestamps, the *start event* and the *end event* of the state, must be contained in the predicate.

These *temporal parameters*, i.e., the timestamps, are an important input for an algorithm that computes the possible causal sequence of events, e.g., to find the *primary event* that caused an *event shower* in an alarm system [28, p. 9]. *Natural language*, which has been developed before the widespread capability to measure the precise time by clocks, provides limited methods to express the temporal order of events by means of the *tense* that is part of the predicate of a basic sentence (the *Zeitwort*). In the DIT model we do not work with the *tense system* of a natural language since we assume that a precise global clock (the GPS) is available that provides the required precise timestamps for recording the instant or the temporal validity of a happening that is expressed by a predicate.

There have been alternative developments that support the temporal reasoning about event sequences, e.g., the development of *temporal logic* [53]. The focus of the original version of temporal logic was on the temporal order of events that can be expressed by the tense system of a natural language without reference to a precise global clock. Later on, temporal logic has been expanded to include reference to a global time [54].

Chapter 8
Data in Real-Time Control Systems

In a real-time control system (RT system), a computer system interacts periodically with an object in the physical environment (often called the *controlled object*) in order to control a production process or to achieve a desired state of the environment. These periodic interactions occur at two different periodic instants:

1. the *instant of observation* (or *sampling point*) when the RT system observes the state of the environment by the use of sensors. At the sampling points the computer system acquires *real-time input data* about the state of the environment.
2. the *instant of actuation* when the RT system outputs the setpoints to the actuators that influence the behavior of the controlled object. The *setpoint output data* that is sent to the actuators must be based on *real-time input data* that is valid at the *instant of use* (i.e., *the time point of actuation*). The duration of the temporal validity interval of the *real-time input data* depends on the dynamics of the environment.

We call the interval between the *sampling instant* and the *instant of actuation* the *response time* of the computer system. The response time is a characteristic parameter for the performance of the RT computer system and can typically vary from less than a millisecond to more than hours, depending on the complexity of the computational tasks and the performance of the available hardware platform. The mean time interval between the *instant of actuation* of the computer system and a noticeable change in the measured value of the controlled object is called the *lag time*. The *lag time* is a characteristic parameter of the controlled object and can vary from less than a microsecond to much more than an hour, depending on the application. The time interval between two successive *sampling instants* is called the *sampling interval*, also called a *frame*.

The following *rules of thumb* give approximate relations that should hold between these three intervals:

© The Author(s), under exclusive license to Springer Nature Switzerland AG 2022   43
H. Kopetz, *Data, Information, and Time*, SpringerBriefs in Computer Science,
https://doi.org/10.1007/978-3-030-96329-3_8

$$sampling\ interval\ =\ 0.1 \times lag\ interval$$
$$response\ interval\ <\ sampling\ interval$$

8.1   Four Real-Time (RT) Applications

In this section we introduce four RT applications to focus on four typical characteristics of a real-time control system. The first application, a *simple temperature control*, shows that in a real-time application it is not sufficient to look solely at the functionality of the software. The second application, *automotive engine control*, shows that in some real-time applications the exact timing of the output signal is of utmost importance. The third application, *control of the stability of a smart electric grid*, shows that a *minimal transmission delay* of the acquired real-time data to a central control room is a critical requirement. The fourth application, *additive manufacturing*, is selected to introduce the notion of a *control data base*, a notion that is referred to in Sect. 9.3 on biological data.

Temperature Control   In the simple closed loop control system of Fig. 8.1 the sensor observes the temperature T of the controlled environment. The controller executes periodically the control program sketched in Fig. 8.1 and outputs the calculated setpoint to switch the relay of the heater to *on* or *off* in order to keep the temperature in the environment around 20°. In this example the *lag interval*—i.e., the time interval until the sensor reacts to the onset of heating—is about 10 mins. It takes the computer less than 10 ms to execute the control program (without the wait statement). In order to extend the sampling interval to 1 min, a wait statement is included in the program shown in Fig. 8.1. The wait statement effects the timing of the control loop but has effect on the calculations within the control program.

Let us discuss the reason for the *wait statement*. If this *statement* were omitted then the *response interval* of the computer (without the wait statement) is 10 ms. In

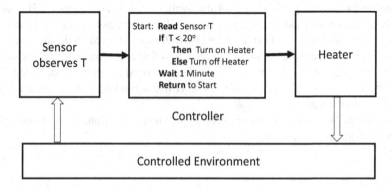

Fig. 8.1 Simple closed loop temperature control system

this case 100 output commands to the relay would be carried out every second. Consider the case when the measured temperature fluctuates around the setpoint of 20°. Then a considerable number of these output commands—let us assume 10%—would cause a switching action of the relay. Since a relay is a mechanical device that *wears out* after—let us assume—1,000,000 switching cycles, the omission of the Wait statement would reduce the *mean time between failures* of the relay from 10,000,000 mins (i.e., about 20 years) to 100,000 s (i.e., about 1 day). This simple example demonstrates that it is not sufficient to look only at the functional correctness of a real-time program.

Automotive Engine Control In the computer-controlled injection of fuel into an automotive engine the precise placement of the *point of actuation* on the timeline is very critical. The fuel injection has to take place at a moment when the angle of the crankshaft is at a precise predetermined position with a tolerance of significantly less than 1 degree. Consider the case where engine revolves with 6000 rpm, i.e., 100 revolutions per second. It takes only 0.01/360 seconds, i.e., it takes the crankshaft only about 30 μs, to move by one degree. In this application, the *point of actuation* must be placed on the timeline with a precision of about 10 μs.

Control of the Stability of a Smart Electric Grid In a stable electric grid the *supply* and *demand* of electric energy are balanced. It is a tremendous challenge for the control engineers to maintain this balance in a *smart grid*, where intermittent decentralized energy sources, such as *photovoltaic panels* and *wind turbines*, provide a significant part of the energy supply. If this balance is disturbed then the grid becomes unstable and, in the worst case, a blackout develops. Such a disturbance can be caused by a reduction of the supply (e.g., clouds cover the sun over the PC panels, no wind), by an increase in demand (e.g., on a cold winter day more energy is required for heating the homes), or by a breakdown of an equipment (e.g., when a tree falls on a power line).

The control of the stability of a smart electric grid requires

1. the synchronized observation of the state of the grid at many distant sensing points in about 10–100 ms intervals [55, p. 22],
2. the swift and predictable transmission of the sensed data to a central control room,
3. the analysis of this data in the central control room to detect the onset of an instability, and,
4. the swift initiation of mitigating actions to bring supply and demand back into balance in case the onset of an instability is detected.

The observations of the state of the grid at selected points are performed by *Phasor Measurement Units (PMU)* that capture the voltage, the current, and the phase angle at periodic globally synchronized GPS time instants (about 10–100 times in every second). The synchronization with the GPS time guarantees that the state of the grid is observed at about the same instant at all relevant locations.

In the control of the stability of the electric grid a small tran*smission delay* **(i.e., the interval between the** *start of sending* **a message at the PMU site and the** *end of receiving this message* **in the distant control room) of the messages containing the PMU data is of utmost importance, since every millisecond counts**.

The smallest possible transmission delay is given by the sum of the *propagation interval* (i.e., the interval it takes from the sending of a bit of a message until this bit arrives at the receiver) and the *transmission interval* (i.e., the interval between sending the first bit and the last bit of a message). The *propagation interval* is determined by the physical distance between a PMU sensor and the control room and cannot be influenced. Given the communication bandwidth, the transmission interval is proportional to the number of bits in the message (the *message length*). The transmission interval can be significantly reduced if a time-triggered protocol is deployed (which eliminates *all waiting times* in the communication system by design) and only the *essential data* (*e-data*—see Sect. 4.2) of a PMU measurement is put into the message. The known *external context* of a global time can be used to further reduce the encoding of the e-data: the *sense instant* and the *PMU identification* do not have to be part of the transmitted data, since they can be recovered from the *instant of arrival of a time-triggered PMU message* at the receiver.

The *received PMU data* and the *topology of the electric grid* are the main parameters for the detection of an onset of an instability in the central control room. In order to receive a satisfying result within a short time, *anytime algorithms* should be used for the analysis of the PMU data in the smart grid (see the following Sect. 8.2).

If the onset of an instability is detected, mitigating actions must be started to either increase the supply or reduce the demand of electric energy. The increase of supply can be achieved by the swift activation of the energy stored in distributed grid-based battery banks, by the start-up of further hydro-electric generators, gas turbines or, in the worst case, by the immediate start-up of emergency generators that are installed in the critical infrastructure, such as hospitals or airports. The reduction of demand can be realized by the selective shutdown of large energy users (brownouts) until a new balance of supply and demand is established.

Additive Manufacturing *Additive Manufacturing* is an umbrella term that covers a number of manufacturing processes, notably 3D printing, that produce three dimensional objects of a given shape by depositing material, predominantly polymers, in a sequence of thin layers, the *slices*, under real-time computer control. In a first phase a 3D model of the desired object is created, e.g., by a computer-aided design (CAD) software package. Such a 3D model can be stored in a special file format, the *stereolithography file format (STL)* [56]. An STL file contains the *generic control database* for the later printing process. In the next phase the *generic STL control database* is transformed to a *concrete control database* that contains the *printing instructions* for every slice. The format of the data in this database is tailored to the specific type of *production machinery*, e.g., the available 3D printer. The real-time computer uses the *concrete control database* to instruct the 3D printer how to move the printing head step-by-step in order to produce, slice by slice, the desired object. The meaning of a data item of the *concrete control database* is given by the physical action of the *production machinery* that is caused by this data item.

8.2   Precision Versus Timeliness of Real-Time Data

In a demanding computer application, such as a closed loop RT control system for *autonomous driving* or the detection of the onset of an instability in the *smart electric grid*, a short execution time of the control algorithms is important. In a control system for autonomous driving, this execution time of the control algorithms can approach the *physical frame duration*, because many sophisticated tasks, such as feature recognition and trajectory planning, must be completed anew during each frame. There are conflicting demands that must be considered when the *physical duration of a frame* is established.

A RT data item that is observed at a *sampling point* at the beginning of frame determines the result of a computation that is used at the *point of actuation* at the end of the frame:

- The shorter the duration of a frame, the more recent (and in consequence the more accurate) is the RT data item that is the basis for the next setpoint.
- The longer the duration of a frame, the more physical time is available for the execution of the control algorithm to calculate the value of the next setpoint.

We call an algorithm that must be executed until completion in order that a valid result is produced a *Worst-Case-Execution-Time* (WCET) Algorithm. The worst-case execution time (WCET) of an algorithm is the longest interval of physical time the algorithm could take to come to completion on the given hardware platform. If a WCET algorithm is interrupted before its WCET, then the (intermediate) result, i.e., the produced value, is useless. In order to arrive at a useful result for all input cases, a control system that deploys WECT algorithms must assure that the *physical duration of a frame* is longer than the WCET on the given hardware platform.

The execution time of an algorithm depends on three factors

- the input data to the algorithm,
- the design of the algorithm and,
- the design and performance of the hardware platform.

Since the WCET is the worst-case execution time of the algorithm, it depends only on the latter two factors. Due to the design of modern hardware, where caches and speculative execution are deployed, the WCET is often significantly longer than the average execution time of an algorithm on the given platform. If the *physical duration of a frame* is established on the basis of the WCET, then on average, the result is ready long before the end of the provided frame. Since the frame length is an input parameter to the algorithm that influences the value of the output, the output value should only be used at the end of the frame.

Fortunately, there exists another class of control algorithms, called *anytime algorithms*, that helps to solve this problem. An anytime algorithm [57] is guaranteed to provide a *satisficing result* long before the *end of frame* and will continually improve this result until the end of frame is reached. A result is a *satisficing result* if it is *adequate* (but not necessarily optimal) in the given situation and meets all safety assertions.

An anytime algorithm consists of a *core segment* followed by an *enhancing segment*. The execution of the core segment is guaranteed to provide the *satisficing* result quickly. Continuous improvements of the satisficing result are provided by the repeated execution of the enhancing segment until the deadline is reached. A good example for an anytime algorithm is *Newton's iterative method* for finding the roots of an equation. Anytime algorithms are widely used in search problems or scene analysis problems.

In the anytime approach, a WCET bound for the core segment must be established. As a consequence, the core segment must deploy algorithms that are amenable to WCET analysis [58]. The size of the time interval between the average execution time of the core segment and the WCET of the core segment is used to improve the quality of the result. The WCET bound for the core segment can be derived either from an analytical analysis of the core segment code of the algorithm or from experimental observations of the execution times of the algorithm on the provided hardware platform (or from both) in the given application context. In a safety critical system, a violation of this WCET bound is tantamount to a serious failure that must be masked by a redundant mechanism.

Characteristic of an anytime algorithm is the *precision error* of the result at the end of a frame, i.e., the instant of interruption. We call the value that is provided in case the algorithm would have all the time needed to run to completion the *precise result*. The *precision error* is the difference between the result provided at the instant of interruption and the precise result. The *precision profile* of an anytime algorithm depicts the dependence of the precision error on the duration of a frame (the provided time for the execution of the anytime algorithm). In most cases, the precision error is significantly reduced in the first few iterations of an anytime algorithm.

The *precision error* of an anytime algorithm must be compared with the *latency error*. The latency error is caused by the fact that the results of the control algorithm are calculated with *past* input values. In the hypothetical case that the execution time of the control algorithm would approach zero, the latency error would disappear. The *latency error* is caused by two different phenomena:

- Reality has *changed* since the last instant of observation. The impact of unidentified or unanticipated processes in the environment (*environmental dynamics*) of an open system increases with the length of the frame.
- Imperfections of the model: The model is not a *true* image for the behavior of reality. For example, nonlinearities that exist in reality have not been properly modeled.

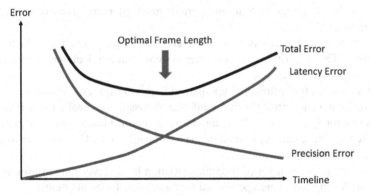

Fig. 8.2 Error of an anytime algorithm as a function of the frame length

The latency error will increase if we move further away from the instant where the *state variables* of the system have been observed, i.e., when the duration of a frame is increased.

If we extend the frame duration for the execution of an anytime algorithm, the *precision error* will be reduced, but the *latency error* will be increased. In a given application there must thus be the *optimal frame duration* where the total error, the sum of the precision error and the latency error, is minimized. Figure 8.2 shows the dependency of the precision error, the latency error, and the total error as a function of the duration of the frame duration [57].

Let us explain the situation by looking at the following example from the domain of automated driving. When analyzing the input from a camera to find relevant features in the picture, there is an inherent conflict between precision and timeliness. Approximate satisficing results that are delivered in time are of higher utility than precise results that arrive too late. If an automated driving system cannot decide whether an obscurity on the road ahead is a shadow or a rock, it is better to brake immediately than to wait until a precise identification of the obscurity is available. In such a situation the provision of an *anytime algorithm* is a good choice. An anytime algorithm is guaranteed to detect an obscurity within its core segment. If there is some time left it can further analyze the obscurity within the current frame to find out if an emergency action is justified. If no time is left to analyze the obscurity, the execution of an emergency action can start immediately.

8.3 Semiautonomous Control Systems

We call a computer control system *semiautonomous*, if under normal circumstances the computer system can control the physical process autonomously, but in case of an exceptional condition, such as the appearance of an *uncovered edge case* or a *failure* of the computer system, an operator must intervene to avoid catastrophic consequences.

An uncovered edge case is a scenario that is not properly covered by the provided algorithms. The majority of the computer systems that are deployed in industry are of the semiautonomous type.

Let us discuss the following hypothetical scenario of a semiautonomous system when *Tom* enters a control booth for automated passport control after arriving at an airport in a foreign country. The computer in the control booth has a camera to take a picture of Tom, a scanner to read the passport page, and a GPS receiver to get the timestamp of the instant *now*.

In the computer is a set of programs (written by a clever human programmer) that provides the following operational *explanations* of the data items:

- what to do with the field that contains the name of Tom?
- what to do with the picture of the passport owner on the scanned passport page?
- what to do with the timestamp for the start of the validity interval of the passport?
- what to do with the timestamp for the end of the validity interval of the passport?

As soon as the data items have been retrieved, the software of the computer manipulates the data according to the rules provided by the programmer.

After entering the control booth, the computer takes a picture of Tom and compares this picture with the picture in the passport in order to establish the authenticity of Tom. It then checks whether the instant *now*, acquired from the GPS, is within the validity interval written in the passport. It then checks the Interpol database to find out in what type of accident Tom was involved. It discovers the car accident of 210,615 and learns that Tom was not guilty in causing the accident. It then opens the exit door of the booth.

If the semiautonomous computer system controlling the process in the control booth runs into an *edge case*, e.g., that the picture in the passport is different from the picture taken by the camera, then a human supervisor is called to handle the situation.

8.4 Fully Autonomous Systems

We call a computer system *fully autonomous*, if the computer system can control the physical process autonomously under *all circumstances*—including unspecified *edge cases* and *internal failures* of the computer system—and avoid catastrophic consequences without the supervision by and the support of an attentive human.

In a fully autonomous safety critical system the computer system has to provide all services that are provided by a human in a semiautonomous system. It must detect an uncovered edge case or an internal failure and bring the physical process to a safe state. It is evident that such a fully autonomous computer system must be partitioned into a number of independent fault-containment units (FCUs) that monitor each other and are assumed to fail independently [30, p. 121]. If a hardware or software failure of a fault-containment unit (FCU) occurs, the failure must be detected and mitigated by the other FCUs of the distributed control system such that catastrophic consequences are avoided.

Let us take the example of a simple function of a fully autonomous driving system (SAE level 4, see ref. [59]) of a car and compare the operation of a human driver with the operation of a fully autonomous computer system.

When a human drives a car and sees a *speed limit sign* he/she checks the speed and brings the car to a speed below the indicated speed limit sign.

The Itom

⟨**subject**⟩	⟨**predicate**⟩	⟨**object**⟩
the speed of the car	should be below	the seen speed limit

is grounded by a human as follows:

- The *subject* is grounded by reading the display of the speed sensor at the dashport in the car.
- the *object* is grounded by the visual recognition of the traffic sign,
- the *predicate* is grounded in the conceptual landscape of the driver based on the explicit and tacit knowledge acquired first in driving school, and then by driving experiences.

When a computer drives a car and identifies a *speed limit sign* it checks the speed and brings the car to a speed below the indicated speed limit.

So, what is the difference if the car is driven by a *human* or by a *computer*?

- In both cases the *subject* (the speed of the car) is grounded by an instrument within the car.
- In case of a human driver, the *object* (the seen speed limit sign) is recognized by autonomous neural processes in the vision subsystem of the human brain and the result, the *indicated speed limit,* is delivered to the *dynamic core* via an input port (see Sect. 4.1) for further conscious processing. In case of a computer driving the car, the object is recognized by the vision subsystem of the computer and delivered to the control software in the computer. There is no substantial *functional difference* between the human driver and the computer with respect to the identification of the object.
- The main difference is in the *predicate*. The human driver brings all explicit and tacit experiences and common sense about driving into play. The predicate in a computerized driving system is grounded in the control algorithms developed by a human programmer who understands the dynamics of a car. The computer executes these algorithms without any *understanding* of what is going on.

Let us now consider an edge case, in which an unreasonable (wrong) speed limit is perceived, e.g., the Itom *"The speed limit is 90 km/h"* instead of *"The speed limit is 30 km/h."* Such an error could be caused by a *mistaken speed limit sign*, by a *bug in the feature detection software*, or by a *hardware failure.* Fault injection experiments with machine learning software have shown that a single bit flip in the hardware, caused by a single event upset (SEU), can result that the Itom *There is a truck ahead* is mistakenly classified as the Itom *There is a bird ahead* [60].

A human driver will detect such an error by looking at the overall context of the traffic scenario and by applying *common sense*. She/he will immediately realize that under the given circumstances the Itom *"The speed limit is 90 km/h"* is in error.

A computerized system, which does not have *common sense*, executes the provided algorithms. In principle, the computer programmer could incorporate all explicit driving experiences into the algorithms, but—at least up to now—cannot formalize the *tacit knowledge* and the *common sense* of a human driver.

Computers manipulate data, i.e., tokens encoded in bit patterns, according to algorithms provided by humans, without any concern for an *understanding* of the full context of the data or the physical effects of the operations.

Chapter 9
Data in Biological Systems

In this short section, we investigate whether the notions of *data*, *information*, and *time* that are at the base of the DIT model can also be applied to biological systems, i.e., *living systems*. But what is *life*? In our tentative view, life is a *process* that

- functions in a physical embodiment that consumes energy and low-structured material from the environment to produce its highly structured embodiment according to a *control database* (a master plan—the *genome*),
- is capable of autonomously producing a new generation of its embodiment, and,
- proceeds unidirectionally in time from the birth to the death of a given embodiment.

9.1 Phases in the Life of a Plant

Let us describe with a few words our simple model about *the process of life* as it unfolds in the development of a plant over time (Fig. 9.1). We use a *plant* as an example of a biological system, because it is widely assumed that plants have no *consciousness*. We distinguish between the following four phases in the life of a plant:

- the dormant phase,
- the germinating phase,
- the growth phase, and,
- the mature phase.

A plant is a multicellular organism that has the ability to carry out photosynthesis for the transformation of the energy of the sunlight into a chemical form that can be used by the biological processes within the plant.

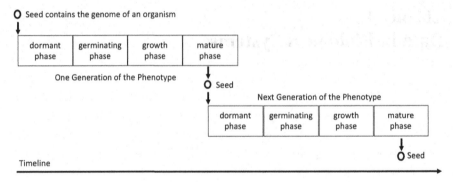

Fig. 9.1 The process of plant life over two generations

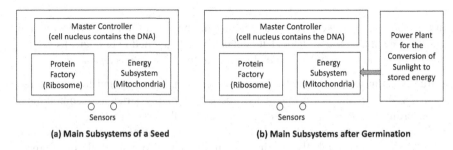

Fig. 9.2 Subsystems of a seed

Dormant Phase The dormant phase of a seed starts with the delivery of the seed to the environment by the previous generation of the embodiment. The seed contains the *genome* in the DNA, i.e., the *master plan* for the construction of the *phenotype*. The seed has a limited reservoir of stored energy and includes sensors to determine the current state of its environment (Fig. 9.2a). Since the seed can stay in the dormant state for a long interval, the energy requirement for the operation of the sensors must be very small. For example, a sensor can consist of an organic molecule that changes its shape as a function of temperature. If the seed senses that the environmental conditions (temperature, humidity, etc.) are favorable for germination, it leaves the *dormant phase* and enters the *germinating phase*.

Germinating Phase After entering the germinating phase the master controller (see Fig. 9.2) selects the part of the DNA (the control database) for the germinating phase. It transforms the relevant sections of the DNA to a form that can be readily used to control the *Protein Factories* (the Ribosomes) in the production of the proteins for the different cell types. The cells multiply by division. The cells for the construction and operation of the *Power Plant* are produced in the germinating phase. Until the *Power Plant* is operational and provides the needed chemical energy, the energy stored in the seed is used to support the life of the organism. The power plant transforms the energy of the sunlight by the process of photosynthesis to a form that can be used by the organism (see Fig. 9.2b). At this point, when the evolving organism is capable of capturing its energy needs from the environment—when a plant has green leaves—the organism enters the growth phase.

Growth Phase During the growth phase the phenotype is gradually constructed under the controls retrieved from the DNA. The omnipotent stem cells have the capability to produce the different cell types that are part of the grown phenotype. The growing organism needs the energy provided by the power plant to develop more and more involved organic structures out of the simply structured material that is acquired from the environment.

Mature Phase After the growth of the plant is complete, the organism is capable of producing the seeds that contain the genetic material (the genome) for the next generation of phenotypes, as shown in Fig. 9.1. The cycle starts again in the next generation of life.

9.2   The *Control Database—The DNA*

The phases of life unfold under the control of a *large control* database (see also Sect. 8.1), the genome, which is contained in a very complex organic molecule, the *Deoxyribonucleic Acid,* abbreviated by DNA. The DNA contains the genetic rules for the growth, the functioning, and the reproduction of a plant or an animal. Every cell of an organism carries the genetic instructions, the DNA, in its cell nucleus.

The DNA is represented by a sequence of base pairs, using four different bases as its building blocks. Three sequential base pairs make up a *codon* which determines the specific amino acid that will be added next in the process of protein synthesis. In order to maintain the integrity of the DNA the *storage structure* of the DNA is very robust. It provides redundancy by storing codons in the form of a double helix of base pairs. The two strands of the double helix are held together by hydrogen bonds among corresponding base pairs.

The process of protein synthesis is executed in the *ribosomes* of a cell under the control of a sequence of codons. It is the temporal order of codons, where every codon encodes one out of about 20 amino acids, that determines the composition and structure of the synthesized protein.

A *ribosome* is a *protein factory.* In order to make the codons accessible to the ribosomes, the coding of the genome is transformed from the robust DNA code to a less robust but better readable single-stranded mRNA (messenger RiboNucleic Acid) code before it leaves the nucleus of its cell. A ribosome links the amino acids identified by the codons of the mRNA in the order specified by the mRNA to form a particular protein. It is estimated that the human body contains more than 100,000 different proteins.

From the point of view of the DIT model, a *codon* is thus a meaningful data item that is grounded in the process of protein synthesis within a cell and controls the manufacturing of proteins in a ribosome.

Let us look at the similarity of *additive manufacturing* (see Sect. 8.1) where an *artifact* is created by a *3D printer* and *biology* where a *protein* is created by a *ribosome* (Fig. 9.3). In both cases the process starts from a generic control database that is transformed to a format that can be used by the production machinery. The meaning of a data item of the *control database* is determined by the physical actions of the production machinery that is caused by this data item. The production machinery does not *understand* the data item. In the domain of computer science, an element of this control database is often called a *data item* while in the domain of biology, an element of this control database is often called an *information item*.

A *unit of hereditary traits* that are specified by the sequence of codons of the respective mRNA (derived from the DNA) is called a *gene*. Every gene is integrated at a particular region of a larger genetic structure, the *chromosome*. Not all genes that are located within the same regions of a chromosome are alike. A gene's name thus denotes a category of functionally related variants of the gene, called *alleles*. Finally, 46 chromosomes form the complete human genome that is contained in the DNA. The DNA that consists of billions of codons is passed from one generation to the next generation with minimal alterations.

The question of how the *control database*, the *DNA,* of a living organism was generated by evolutionary processes in the first place is outside the scope of the DIT model and subject of intense research.

The existence of living organisms is very much dependent on the proper physical environment, such as temperature, composition of the atmosphere, and availability of sunlight as a primary energy source. The sunlight provides the energy for the growth of the plants. The plants store this energy in the form of starch, which is a complex carbohydrate that can be broken down to glucose. The glucose is consumed by the *mitochondria* in the cells of a plant to provide the chemical energy to the biological processes in an appropriate form. Animals get their energy indirectly from the sun—they consume the starch that is contained in the food produced by plants.

	Protein Synthesis	3D Printing
Generic Control Data Base	DNA	*stereolithography file format (STL)*
Manufacturing Instructions	mRNA	Concrete Control Database
Production Machinery	Ribosome	3 D Printer

Fig. 9.3 Comparison of a protein synthesis with 3D printing (see Sect. 8.1)

9.3 Data in Computers, Plants, and Human Communication

In this section we try to compare the characteristics and the differences in the notion of a *data item* (of the DIT model) that is involved in the operation of a computer, the growth of a plant, or in human communication using natural language. In the DIT model the term *data item* denotes a symbol where the *signifier* is the name of the data item and the *signified* is the meaning of the data item. When no human is directly involved in a phenomenon, the meaning of a data item can be deduced from the *concrete operations* that this data item is involved in (operational definition).

Figure 9.4 looks at the term *data item* from the viewpoint of a computer application, the growth of a plant, and from the viewpoint of human communication.

We are aware that our use of the terms *data* and *information* is sometimes different from the use of these terms in colloquial language. In colloquial language the uses of the words data and information are occasionally inconsistent. In the DIT model the term *information* is only used when humans communicate in natural language, using grounded words. A natural language statement makes *sense* to a human who listens to and *understands* this statement. This *sense* is captured in the notion of an *information item (Itom)*. Computers (and plants) do not *understand*; they execute operations that are given to them, either by human programmers in the form of a program or by the evolutionary process in the form of the genome.

	Computer	Plant	Human
Signifier	variable	codon	word
Signified	a specific value	a specific amino acid	concept in the human mind
Meaning of the *signified* derived from	its use in a program	its use in protein synthesis	concept formation
Physical Embodiment generated by	Human	Nature	Nature
Modification of the Physical Embodiment by its use	No	Yes	Yes
Reproduction capability	No	Yes	Yes

Fig. 9.4 Data item as used by a computer, a plant, and in communication among humans

Chapter 10
Generation and Explanation of Data

In the DIT model we consider the *signifier* of a *data item* as a pattern that denotes *a symbol* in the physical world. The *signified* of the symbol depends on the given environment. If the data item is intended for a human, the *signified* is an already formed concept in the human mind. If the data item is used by a computer, the *signified* is a value housed in a token where the meaning of the value is determined by the set of operations that the name of the value—the variable name—is involved in. This set of operations has been designed by a human programmer who understands the meaning of the involved tokens.

An *Itom* is the sense of a natural language proposition. It identifies the *entity* that is involved, describes *the property of interest,* and contains a *data item* that is usually a *value* for the further qualification of the property. If the property can change in the IOD the Itom must include temporal parameters to indicate the instant of the observation of the entity or the validity interval of the values. As noted above, a proposition is only meaningful to a human if all fields of the proposition are grounded in the mind of the reader. We have to find a representation of an Itom where all fields are meaningful to a human user in the given cultural context.

10.1 Generation of Data

The *generation of data* starts with an observation of that part of the state of a phenomenon in reality that is required to meet a given purpose at a given instant of time. The sense of an observation is captured in the respective Itom. Let us look at the four parts of the Itom in some detail:

- **Identification of an entity:** Since there can be an unbounded number of entities in the CSTD, we have to identify an entity or categorize the entities in order to restrict the number of entities.

H. Kopetz, *Data, Information, and Time*, SpringerBriefs in Computer Science, https://doi.org/10.1007/978-3-030-96329-3_10

- **Identification of a property:** The property must be precisely specified to avoid any misunderstandings. If the property specification changes in the IoD, then the value will probably change as well.
- **Value of the property:** This is often a literal (e.g., a string of digits) representing a numeric value. The measuring units of the numeric value must be included in the property specification.
- **Timestamp of the observation of the phenomenon:** The instant of observation of the entity in the dynamic environment must be stored in a timestamp. In a situation where the value of the property is used at some later time for a real-time control action, a second timestamp for the end of the validity time of the observation must be part of the temporal data.

Data Acquisition by a Human The acquisition of sense-data items by the human senses is supported by an elaborate autonomous data preprocessing and categorization system in the human brain, such that high-level concepts and the associated parameters of an observed scene are provided at the input port to the dynamic core (see Sect. 4.1). This autonomous data categorization system is part of the intuitive-experiential subsystem of the *cognitive landscape* [28, p. 32]. The result of the data acquisition process can be described by an Itom that is represented in an understandable form to the human mind.

A human can place a *value* into many different data structures. The database schema (see Sect. 7.1) can explain the value by using grounded words in the description of the schema.

For example, if we are interested in the change of a single property over time, we can provide a table or graph depicting the value over time. In many cases, the *number of entities in a category* is presented as a time series in the form of a table (Fig. 7.2) or a graph (Fig. 10.1). Care must be taken that the properties that define the category are not changed during the considered time frame.

Let us look at the following example of an Itom as a function of time. The Itom

⟨Subject⟩	⟨predicate⟩	⟨object⟩
The category of Covid19 infected persons	*has the indicated number of members*	125788 *on* 21 11 15

This Itom is recorded every day since February 15, 2020, and the result is displayed in the graph as shown in Fig. 10.1.

There is a problem with this time series of values: The definition of the category *Covid 19 infected persons* has changed during the IoD. In the beginning of the pandemic, a person was considered *Covid 19 infected* if the person showed symptoms of the disease. Later on, people who did not show symptoms but have been tested positive were also included in the category *Covid 19 infected*. During the pandemic the test coverage (percentage of the population tested) and the selection of the person that were tested also changed. If the meaning of the words that define the

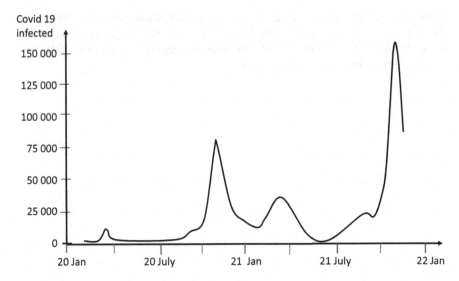

Fig. 10.1 Number of active COVID 19 patients in Austria

category of interest change during the interval of a time series, then the shown numbers in the *time series set of values* are of limited worth.

Data Acquisition by a Computer A computerized data logger can autonomously record desired data items over time. The design of such a system is developed by human engineers. A human-designed sensor transforms the physical quantity to a *sensor-specific bit pattern.* This bit pattern is converted to a standardized form by a program developed by a human programmer who understands the operation of the sensor. The *numeric value* that expresses the acquired value is then used in further computations.

10.2   Explanation of Data

The explanation of the data is somehow the inverse of the generation of the data. Care must be taken that the context of explanation of data is the same as the context of the generation of data. This is of particular importance when the *change of context* between the ins*tant of data generation* and *instant of data explanation* has an effect on the explanation of the data. At the human-machine interface (HMI) the representation of the *values of interest* must be framed by an explanation that is grounded in the mind of the human reader. Also, the measurement units of values must be familiar to the intended clientele of the Itom.

In Sect. 6.1 on human communication we elaborated on the transmission of an Itom from a human sender to a human receiver (Fig. 6.1) and declared that the explanation of the data must be derived from the inner context in the dynamic core in the brain of the receiver. A good agreement between the inner context of the sender at the time of generating data and the inner context of the receiver at the time of explanation of the data is crucial for the assurance that the *explanation of the data* is compatible with the *generation of the data.*

Chapter 11
Consequences for System Design

In the world of engineering, the *practical usefulness* of a model for building better systems is more relevant than its irrefutable correctness. In this final section we provide some short examples to show how the insights gained from the DIT model can help in the design of *more useful* computer systems.

11.1 Specification Dilemma

The fact that the precise meaning of a natural language word is subjective and unique to a single person and may thus differ among different persons is the cause of the *specification dilemma* that can lead to misunderstandings in the specifications of the intended behavior of a computer system. The proposal to use tokens of a *formal symbolic language* is only a partial solution of this specification dilemma. Although the relations among the tokens of a formal language are precisely defined, the tokens themselves are not grounded in the real world. There are a number of situations, where the use of natural language is unavoidable, such as in the specification of

- the purpose of a system,
- the grounding of the symbols or,
- the interfaces between cyberspace and the real world.

However, the data interfaces within and between the computers in cyberspace can and should be formally specified.

The specification dilemma can be mitigated by providing at the beginning of a large project a comprehensive glossary of the meaning of all special natural language terms that are used in the project. This glossary must be consistently updated by the documentation manager. The project team must be asked to report any modification in the meaning of a term to the documentation manager.

H. Kopetz, *Data, Information, and Time*, SpringerBriefs in Computer Science,
https://doi.org/10.1007/978-3-030-96329-3_11

11.2   Human-Machine Interface (HMI) Design

When a *variable* is displayed at an interface to a human user, the display must include the *value* and the *explanation of the value* in an appropriate *display format*, such that the human user can grasp the *meaning of the value* with a minimal mental load. A *display format* is appropriate, if the display form of the variable takes account of the experience, the cultural background, the work profile, and the work environment—i.e., the *internal* and *external contexts*—of the clientele of the Itom. A novice user will appreciate a more detailed explanation than an experienced user. This suggests that a user should be able to change the display form according to his background, experience, and liking. The display should also inform about the importance of the variable in the current work situation, e.g., by using a widely appreciated color code. The complexity reduction principle of *divide and conquer* [30, p.77] suggests that the *generation of the result data* and the *explanation of the variable* should be implemented in two nearly independent subsystems. A thorough study of the assumed conceptual landscape and the work environment of the intended clientele of the variable is a good starting point for designing the appropriate display form for a variable at the HMI.

For example, I am annoyed at the display form of a variable at the dashboard of my car, since the static explanation of the data, a picture, is larger and has a more prominent form than the dynamic value that is of interest to me.

11.3   Benefits of a Global Time

The DIT model requires a global time in order to arrive at a *non-tensed design*. There are many situations in a real-time computer design, where the known availability of a global time in each node of a distributed computer system can be used to improve the design.

1. The availability of a global time is a prerequisite for the implementation of time-triggered communication protocols. The most significant advantage of a time-triggered communication protocol is the unidirectional control flow from the sender of a message to the receiver of a message. This is in contrast to the widely used event-triggered protocols (such as, e.g., a positive acknowledgment or retransmission protocol—PAR) which require a bidirectional control flow. A unidirectional control flow avoids a failure propagation of a faulty receiver back to a correct sender *by design* and thus improves the reliability and reduces the complexity of a system. Since, in a time-triggered communication system, the receiver knows a priori when a message is supposed to arrive, the receiver can detect a failure in the communication without any involvement of the sender.
2. The responsiveness of a distributed real-time computer system can be improved if the availability of the global time in each node of the computer is used to

synchronize the sending of a message with the receiving and the interpretation of the message, since no intermediate buffering of real-time messages is necessary.

3. Fault-tolerant clock synchronization can be integrated within a time-triggered protocol. A good example is the time-triggered protocol TTP [61] which is in practical use in safety-critical systems in the aero-space domain. TTP realizes a fault-tolerant clock synchronization without any explicit exchange of synchronization messages by taking advantage of the global time and the temporal properties of the time-triggered message transport. By measuring the deviations between the actual arrival times of the time-triggered messages from the a priori known expected arrival times at the receiver of every message, the needed input data for the execution of a fault-tolerant clock synchronization algorithm is collected locally without any load on the transport system.

4. The availability of a global time can be used to establish an upper limit on the maximum load on the real-time communication in an alarm monitoring system. It thus leads to predictable behavior in a peak load scenario [30, p.96].

11.4 Reduction of Context Data (c-Data) in Data Transmission

In many cyber-physical systems, the considered space-time domain (the CSTD) is fairly stable and the static outer contexts of the sender and the receiver of a message can be aligned a priori. It is then possible to put solely the *e-data (essential data)* of an Itom into a real-time message. This reduces the length and transmission time of the real-time message and makes it possible to increase the speed and quality of a control loop.

This technique is illustrated by the following funny episode: A group of friends, sitting in a pub, shout numbers at each other. Some numbers cause the group to start laughing, while other numbers are considered boring. A newcomer watches the group for a while and then asks "What is the meaning of a number?" He is being told that every number refers to one of a set of jokes that all friends know. They only laugh at good jokes, not at boring jokes.

11.5 Partitioning of a Safety-Critical Control System

In Chap. 6 we have discussed the differences between a semiautonomous and a fully autonomous safety-critical computer control system. The chasm between these two types of systems is wide and deep. In a semiautonomous control system, a competent human with explicit and tacit experience encoded in his/her conceptual landscape judges a scenario from a wide perspective and finds creative new solutions to detect and mitigate a new *edge case*. In a fully autonomous safety-critical computer system, these challenging services of failure detection and failure mitigation must be provided by a distributed computer system. Replacing the intelligent information processing services of a human by a data processing machine is a very challenging endeavor.

The differences start at the highest level of the system architecture. While in a semiautonomous system the services of the computer can be implemented in a single monolithic architecture, the design of a fully autonomous control system requires the realization of a distributed computer architecture with independent fault-containment units (FCU) that monitor each other's operation and mitigate a detected failure in order to avoid catastrophic consequences. The implementation of redundancy and design diversity to detect and handle hardware failures and unavoidable design errors in complex software is essential.

The difficult task of partitioning a large RT control system, such as the computer control systems in a car, into nearly independent subsystems that form independent fault-containment units can be supported by the visualization of the unidirectional and bidirectional dependencies and timing relations among the different entities in the form of a *large knowledge graph* (see Sect. 7.2). Unidirectional dependencies can be identified and implemented with time-triggered protocols that ensure that a failure of the receiver of a message will have no effect on the sender. The visual and computational analysis of such a knowledge graph will suggest the lines where the knowledge graph can be decomposed into nearly independent subgraphs with minimal interfaces among the subgraphs.

A detailed discussion of some of these issues is contained in [30, pp. 121–123].

Chapter 12
Conclusions

The Data, Information, and Time (DIT) model makes a clear distinction between the terms *data* and *information* and illustrates how the *meaning of a data item* and the *sense of a proposition* can change over time.

In human communication, the signifier of a *data item* points to a concept in the conceptual landscape (in the human mind) of an attentive human and thus acquires *meaning*. The connection between the signifier and signified is provided by the current internal and external contexts in the minds of the involved humans and explains the meaning of the signifier. Because contexts can change over time, a data item can change its meaning as time flows. In computer communication (and processing) a data item is a token name that denotes a meaningless token that holds a value and can be a part of many relations to other meaningless tokens, thus forming a part of a token system. Computers exchange and process meaningless tokens according to algorithms provided by a human programmer. At the interface of cyberspace to the real world, the meaningless tokens must be grounded in reality either by the assignment of meaningful words to the tokens or by linking the tokens to things in the world by a process control interface.

An *information item*, called *Itom*, is the *sense* of a natural language proposition that contains meaningful data items. The same *sense of a proposition* (the *idea* expressed by the proposition) can be expressed in the physical world by different verbal forms or languages, depending on the cultural and personal context of the involved humans. Since the predicate of a proposition is tensed and the meaning of the data items that are part of a proposition can change over time, the sense of the proposition can also change over time. An Itom can be visualized as a meaningful timed link—*a timed predicate*—in a knowledge graph that connects two meaningful entities. Humans think, process, and communicate in the form of *Itoms* (information items). A variable in a computer program that has a meaningful name can be considered an Itom that makes sense to a human: the variable name refers to a concept that denotes a property of an entity and the value refines this property.

H. Kopetz, *Data, Information, and Time*, SpringerBriefs in Computer Science, https://doi.org/10.1007/978-3-030-96329-3_12

In the final part of this work we give hints how the insights gained from the understanding of the DIT model can help to improve the design of computer systems.

Glossary[1]

Algorithm A sequence of formally defined instructions, often embodied in a computer program, that specifies precise relations among tokens. [Sect. 6.3]

C-Data *Context* Data. [Sect. 4.2]

Category A set of *entities* that share a number of chosen static *properties* and carry a *name*. [Sect. 3.2]

Codon Three sequential base pairs of the DNA. A codon determines the specific amino acid that will be added next in the process of protein synthesis. [Sect. 9.2]

Concept A unit of thought. [Chap. 2]

Conceptual Landscape The totality of all *concepts*, relations among the *concepts*, and *mental models* in the mind of a human. [Chap. 2]

Considered Space-Time Domain A subspace of the four-dimensional space-time domain delimited by the *Universe of Discourse (UoD)* and the *Interval of Discourse (IoD)*. [Sect. 3.2]

Construct A notion created by the human mind to capture an abstract idea. [Sect. 3.2]

Context Data The static *properties* of the *entities* in *the considered space-time domain* that are of relevance in a given communication act (Essential data). [Sect. 4.2]

Context The context of an idea or *event* is the general situation that relates to it, and which helps it to be understood (from *Collins Dictionary*). [Sect. 3.2]

CSTD Considered Space-Time Domain. [Sect. 3.2]

Data ITEM In the DIT model a data ITEM is a symbol that consists of a *signifier* and a *signified*. The *signifier*—the *name* of the *symbol* (e.g., a *word* or variable name)—is the physical pattern that represents the data ITEM in the physical world. In human communication the *signified* of this *symbol* is the meaning of the data ITEM, determined by the *concept* in the mind of an attentive human receiver. In a computer *system* the *signified* of this *symbol* is the *value* housed by a *token* that is operationally explained by the use of the token name in the computer program (operational definition). [Sect. 6.3]

© The Author(s), under exclusive license to Springer Nature Switzerland AG 2022
H. Kopetz, *Data, Information, and Time*, SpringerBriefs in Computer Science,
https://doi.org/10.1007/978-3-030-96329-3

Database Schema The framework for the organization, the access, and the explanation of the stored *values* in a database. [Sect. 7.1]

Database An organized collection of data stored and accessed electronically from a computer system (from Wikipedia). [Sect. 7.1]

Degenerate From the point of view of the DIT model an Itom is *degenerate* if the required temporal information is missing. [Sect. 6.3]

DIT Model The Data, Information, and Time (DIT) Model. [Chap. 2]

Dynamic Core The neural correlate of consciousness in the thalamocortical *system* of the human brain. It carries out a single sequential conscious neural *process* at any one time. [Sect. 4.1]

E-Data Essential Data. [Sect. 4.2]

Entity An animate or inanimate thing that exists in reality or a *construct*. [Sect. 3.2]

Essential Data The dynamic *properties* of the *entities* in the *considered space-time domain* (CSTD) that are of relevance in a given communication act (Context data). [Sect. 4.2]

Event An *event* is a *process* that is shorter than the *granularity* of the chosen clock. [Sect. 3.1]

Global Positioning System A global navigation satellite *system* that provides geo-location and time data to a *GPS* receiver. [Sect. 3.1]

GPS *Global Positioning System.* [Sect. 3.1]

Granularity of a Digital Clock The interval between two consecutive *ticks* of a digital clock. The measurement of the granularity requires a reference clock with a much finer granularity (see [27, p. 53]). [Sect. 3.1]

Grounding The term *grounding* denotes the assignment of a meaningful *word* to a meaningless *token*. [Sect. 3.3]

Happening An umbrella term that includes an *event*, a *state*, or a *process*. [Sect. 3.1]

Inner Context The *inner context* in the mind of a conscious human consists of those parts of the *conceptual landscape* in the human brain that are related to the meaning of a *word* and the current perceptions of relevant *events* in the physical environment, i.e., the *outer context*, that are delivered to the *conceptual landscape* by the human senses. [Sect. 3.2]

Instant A cut of the timeline. [Sect. 3.1]

Interval of Discourse The interval on the timeline that is considered in the given discourse. [Sect. 3.2]

IOD Interval of Discourse. [Sect. 3.2]

ITOM A unit of information. The *sense* of a *proposition* that consists of meaningful *data items*. [Sect. 5.4]

Knowledge Graph In the DIT model a *knowledge graph* is a graphical structure that depicts the *entities* of the *considered space-time domain* as nodes and a relationship among entities as links between related nodes. In a *DIT knowledge graph* all *entities* and links must be *grounded* by naming them with meaningful *words* and the links must be annotated with temporal parameters to denote when the link is temporally valid on the timeline. [Sect. 7.2]

Literal A *signifier* where the gestalt of the *signifier* indicates unambiguously the *signified* in the given cultural environment. [Sect. 3.3]

Mental Model A *model* in the mind of a human that consists of *concepts* and relations among *concepts*. [Sect. 3.4]

Model A *model* is an *abstraction* of a phenomenon that leaves out the many details of the phenomenon that are not considered relevant for the given purpose of the *model*. [Sect. 3.4]

Name A name is a term used for identification. A name can identify a class or *category* of *entities*, or a single *entity*, either uniquely or within a given *context* (from Wikipedia). [Sect. 3.1]

Outer Context The *outer context* of a *word* or an *action* is the objective reality in the current situation. It is determined by the prevailing physical, cultural, and social environment. [Sect. 3.2]

Phasor Measurement Unit A sensor that measures the magnitude and the phase angle of an electrical quantity, such as a voltage or a current, at a given instant. [Sect. 8.1]

PMU Phasor Measurement Unit. [Sect. 8.1]

Process An activity that starts at an *instant* and terminates at an *instant*. [Sect. 3.1]

Proper Name A *signifier* that has a unique *entity* as its signified, e.g., a specific person or a unique thing in the world of the given *CSTD*. [Sect. 3.3]

Property A characteristic feature of an *entity*. [Sect. 3.2]

Proposition A natural language sentence that consists of three phrases, a *subject phrase*, a *predicate phrase*, and an *object phrase*. [Sect. 5.2]

RDF Triple *Resource Description Framework*. [Sect. 7.3]

Resource Description Framework The identification of the three *data items* of a *proposition* by uniform resource identifiers is called a *triple* of the Resource Description Framework, abbreviated by RDF triple. [Sect. 7.3]

Scientific Realism A philosophical position that posits that reality exists independently of an observer. [Chap. 3]

Sense The sense of a proposition is the idea expressed by a *proposition* consisting of meaningful *words*. [Sect. 4.1]

Signified The something that is denoted by the *signifier* of a *symbol*. [Sect. 3.3]

Signifier The physical appearance of a *symbol*. [Sect. 3.3]

State The *properties* of a *system* that have a constant value during an identified interval. [Sect. 3.1]

Symbol A sign that signifies something. The appearance of the *symbol* is called the *signifier* of the *symbol* and the something is called the *signified*. [Sect. 3.3]

System A system is a collection of related *entities* that forms a whole. [Sect. 3.1]

Tense A verbal form that specifies the time of the action or *state* expressed by the verb. [Sect. 5.2]

Theory of Neuronal Group Selection A theory of consciousness that considers consciousness as an *emergent property* as a consequence of the intense interactions among a very large number of neurons in the *dynamic core* of the human brain.

Tick of a Digital Clock One of a sequence of regular time-signs produced by a digital clock. The ticks of a digital clock are numbered, starting with zero at the beginning of an epoch. In the DIT *model* it is assumed that the ticks of the clocks are synchronized with UTC and are numbered according to UTC. [Sect. 3.1]

Timestamp of an Event The *tick* number assigned to the *ticks of a digital clock* that follows the considered event. [Sect. 3.1]

TNGS *Theory of Neuronal Group Selection.* [Sect. 4.1]

Token A meaningless placeholder in the world of *constructs* that can hold a *value* and can take part in a set of relations. [Sect. 3.3]

Uniform Resource Identifier A unique identifier of a resource on the Internet. [Sect. 7.3]

Universal Time Coordinated Universal Time Coordinated is a widely used time standard for measuring the progress of time. [Sect. 3.1]

Universe of Discourse The *set of entities* and the relations among the *entities* in the considered environment. [Sect. 3.2]

UOD *Universe of Discourse.* [Sect. 3.2]

UTC *Universal Time Coordinated.* [Sect. 3.2]

Value The characterization of a *property* of an *entity*. [Sect. 3.2] The something stored in a data structure and explained by the *database schema*. [Sect. 7.1]

Word A natural language *symbol* consisting of a stream of sounds or a sequence of letters as its *signifier* and a *concept* in the mind of a human, who is part of the language community, as its *signified*. A meaningful word is a data ITEM. [Sect. 5.1]

References

1. Randell, B.: Newcastle International Seminars on the Teaching of Computer Science. URL: http://homepages.cs.ncl.ac.uk/brian.randell/Seminars/2001. Accessed 20 Nov 2021
2. Kent, W.: Data and Reality. North Holland Publishing Company, Amsterdam (1978)
3. Zins, C.: Conceptual approaches for defining data, information and knowledge. J. Am. Soc. Inf. Sci. Technol. **58**(4), 479–493 (2007)
4. Capurro, R.: Ein Beitrag zur etymologischen und ideengeschichtlichen Begründung des Informationsbegriffs. Dissertation an der Universität Düsseldorf. KG Sauer Verlag, München (1978)
5. Dretske, F.: Knowledge and the Flow of Information. CSL Publications, Stanford (1999)
6. Bates, M.J.: Information and knowledge: an evolutionary framework for information science. Inf. Res. **10**(4), n4 (2005)
7. Lombardi, O., Holik, F., Vanni, L.: What is Shannon information? Synthese. **193**, 1983–2012 (2016). https://doi.org/10.1007/s11229-015-0824-z
8. Shannon, C.E.: In: Sloane, N.J.A., Wyner, A.D. (eds.) Collected Papers. IEEE Computer Society Press, Los Alamos, CA (1948)
9. Cherry, C.: On Human Communication, 2nd edn. MIT Press, Cambridge (1966)
10. Shannon, C.: In: Sloane, N., Wyner, A. (eds.) Collected Papers. IEEE Press, New York (1993)
11. Bar-Hillel, Y., Carnap, R.: An outline of a theory of semantic information. In: Hillel, B. (ed.) Language and Information, pp. 221–274. Addison Wesley, Boston (1964)
12. Floridi, L.: Is semantic information meaningful data? Philos. Phenomenol. Res. **60**(2), 351–370 (2005)
13. Frege, G.: Sense and reference. In: Philosophical Review, vol. 3, pp. 209–230. Duke University Press, Duke (1948)
14. Lyons, J.: Semantics 2. Cambridge University Press, Cambridge (1977)
15. Mealy, G.: Another look at data. In: Proceeding of the Fall Joint Computer Conference, pp. 525–534. AFIPS, Las Vegas (1967)
16. Wittgenstein, L.: Philosophical Investigations. Blackwell Publishing, Oxford. Reprint (2003)
17. Popper, K.: Three worlds. In: The Tanner Lecture on Human Values. Univ. of Michigan, Michigan (1978) URL: https://tannerlectures.utah.edu/_documents/a-to-z/p/popper80.pdf.1978
18. Edelman, G.M., Tononi, G.: A Universe of Consciousness. Basic Books, New York (2000)
19. Koch, C.: The Quest for Consciousness. Roberts and Company Publishers, Englewood (2004)
20. Rushby, J.: On Mechanisms for Shared Intentionality and Speculation on Rationality and Consciousness. Computer Science Laboratory, SRI International, Menlo Park (2020)

21. Johnson, M.: The Body in the Mind. University of Chicago Press, Chicago (1974)
22. Lackoff, G.: Women, Fire, and Dangerous Things. The University of Chicago Press (1987)
23. Chakravartty, A.: Scientific realism. In: Stanford Encyclopedia of Philosophy. Stanford University, Stanford (2017)
24. Vygotski, S.: Thought and Language. MIT Press, Boston (1962)
25. Boulding, K.E.: The Image. Ann Arbor Paperbacks (1961)
26. English Club 21.URL: https://www.englishclub.com/grammar/verb-tenses-tense-time.htm. Accessed 10 Nov 2021
27. Michaelis, L.A.: Tense in English. In: Aarts, B., McMahon, A. (eds.) Handbook of English Linguistics, pp. 221–243. Blackwell Publishing Inc., Oxford (2006)
28. Kopetz, H.: Real-Time Systems–Design Principles for Distributed Embedded Applications. Springer Verlag, Cham (2011)
29. Kopetz, H.: Sparse time versus dense time in distributed real-time systems. In: Proc. Int. Conf. On Distributed Computer System (1992) URL: https://www.win.tue.nl/~johanl/educ/2Q341/Clocks%20synchronization/1992-kopetz.pdf
30. Kopetz, H.: Simplicity Is Complex—Foundations of Cyber-Physical System Design. Springer Nature, Cham (2019)
31. Harnad, S.: The symbol grounding problem. Phys. D: Non-Linear Phenom. **42**(1–3), 335–346 (1990)
32. Johnson-Laird, P.N.: Mental Models. Cambridge University Press, Cambridge (1983)
33. Craik, K.: The Nature of Explanation. Cambridge University Press, Cambridge (1967)
34. Khalifa, K.: Understanding, Explanation and Scientific Knowledge. Cambridge University Press, Cambridge (2017)
35. Searle, J.R.: The Rediscovery of the Mind. MIT Press, Boston (1992)
36. Edelman, G.M.: Bright Air, Brilliant Fire—On the Matter of the Mind. Basic Books, New York (1992)
37. Darwin, C.: The Origin of Species. Penguin Books, London. originally published in (1859)
38. Sarawagi, S.: Information Extraction. Now Publishers Inc., Boston Delft (2008)
39. Devlin, J. et al. BERT: Pre-training of Deep Bidirectional Transformers for Language Understanding. URL: https://arxiv.org/pdf/1810.04805.pdf&usg=ALkJrhhzxlCL6yTht2BRmH9atgvKFxHsxQ Accessed 28 Nov 2021
40. Hayakawa, S.I.: Language in Thought and Action. Houghton Mifflin Harcourt Publishing Company, Houghton (1941)
41. Lackoff, G., Johnson, M.: Metaphors we Live by. The University of Chicago Press (2003)
42. Lackoff, G., Nunes, R.E.: Where Mathematics Comes from. Basic Books, New York (2000)
43. Harnad, S.: Computation is just interpretable symbol manipulation. Cognition Isn't. Minds and Machines. **4**, 379–390 (1994)
44. Glanzberg, M.: Truth. Stanford Encylopedia of Philosophy, Stanford, USA. (2018) URL: https://plato.stanford.edu/entries/truth/. Accessed 12 Nov 2021
45. Grasse, P.P.: La reconstruction du nid et les coordinations interindiviuelles chez Bellicositermes natalensis et Cubitermes sp. La theorie de la stigmergie. Insectes Sociaux Vo. **6**, 41–83 (1959)
46. Schneider, E.W.: Course Modularization Applied: The Interface System and Its Implications For Sequence Control and Data Analysis. Association for the Development of Instructional Systems (ADIS), Chicago, IL (1972)
47. Hetherington, S.: Knowledge and the Gettier Problem. Cambridge University Press, Cambridge (2016)
48. Singhal, A.: Introducing the Knowledge Graph: Things not Strings. URL: https://blog.google/products/search/introducing-knowledge-graph-things-not/. Accessed 20 Nov 2021
49. Sullivah, D.: A Reintroduction of our Knowledge Graph and Knowledge Panels. URL: https://blog.google/products/search/about-knowledge-graph-and-knowledge-panels. Accessed 20 Nov 2021

50. Ehrlinger, L, ND Wöß, W. Towards a Definition of a Knowledge Graph. URL: http://citeseerx.ist.psu.edu/viewdoc/download?doi=10.1.1.1054.8298&rep=rep1&type=pdf Accessed 11 Nov 2021

51. Kazemi, S.M., et al.: Representation learning for dynamic graphs: a survey. J. Mach. Learn. Res. **21**, 1–73 (2020)

52. Russom, P.: Big Data Analytics. URL: https://vivomente.com/wp-content/uploads/2016/04/big-data-analytics-white-paper.pdf. Accessed on 12 Aug 2021. 2011

53. Pnueli, A.: The temporal logic of programs. In: 18th Annual Symposium on Foundations of Computer Science, pp. 46–57. IEEE Press, Piscataway (1977)

54. Koymans, R.: Specifying real-time properties with metric temporal logic. Real-Time Systems. **2**, 255–299 (1990) Springer Verlag

55. Ramamritham, K., et al.: Energy Management, a Computational Approach. World Scientific, Singapore (2022)

56. All3DP.: STL File Format: Everything you need to know. URL: https://all3dp.com/1/stl-file-format-3d-printing/. Accessed 23 Nov 2021

57. Kopetz, H.: Anytime algorithms in time-triggered control systems. In: Lohstroh, M., et al. (eds.) *Principles of Modeling*, pp. 326–335. Springer Verlag, Cham (2018) Springer LNCS 10760

58. Wilhelm, R., et al.: The worst-case execution time problem—overview of methods and survey of tools. ACM Trans. Embedded Comp. Syst. **7**(3), 1–53 (2008)

59. SAE, Standard J3016: Surface Vehicle Recommended Practice. SAE International, Warrendale (2018)

60. Li, G., et al.: Understanding error propagation in deep learning neural networks (DNN) accelerators and applications. In: Proc. of the International Conference for High Performance Computing, Networking, Storage and Analysis, pp. 1–12. ACM Press (2017)

61. Kopetz, H., Gruensteidl, G.: TTP-A time-triggered protocol for fault-tolerant real-time systems. In: Proc. of FTCS, vol. 23, pp. 524–532. IEEE Press (1993)

62. Johnson, M.: The Body in the Mind. The University of Chicago Press, Chicago, USA (1987)

63. Kazemi, S.M., et al.: Representation Learning for Dynamic Graphs, A Survey. Journal of Machine Learning, Vol 21, pp. 1–73, 2020 URL: https://doi.org/10.48550/arXiv.1905.11485

Printed in the United States
by Baker & Taylor Publisher Services